Journeys Become a Life

Discovering Meaning & Connection
Living & Traveling Abroad

Susan Wilson Bowditch

Front Cover Art: "Integration," fiber art by Susan Bowditch.
The cover art symbolically represents the last stage of cultural sensitivity, from a model by Dr. Milton Bennet, academic and cross-cultural trainer. Using scraps of cloth from clothes sewn in various countries between 1964 and 2006, the author created triangles in separate colors for each of seven wall pieces. The wall pieces represented the different stages a person goes through in another country, demonstrating the progression from ethnocentrism to ethno-relativity. This last piece in the series stands for "Integration of Cultural Differences," when a person can finally understand and feel at home interacting in a culture not original to them. The series was donated to Research Triangle International and hung in Peace Hall, Durham, North Carolina, 2009.

Photos: from the author's personal collection.

Bowditch, Susan Wilson
Journeys Become a Life/Susan Wilson Bowditch
p. 256
1. Biography & Autobiography–General.
I. Title.

ISBN: 978-1-0881-8172-0

Published by:
Windrift Valley Designs
Topsham, Maine

Printed in the United States of America

First Just Write Books Edition 2023
First Windrift Valley Designs Edition 2023

Dedicated with much love
To my grandchildren, Kian and Saskia,
For whom this was written;
and
To my adult kids, Windi and Sean,
Who joined me for part of my journeys,
Changing their lives, I believe, in important ways;
And
Especially to Nate,
Who was a significant part of most journeys,
And shared his life with me.

The author with one of her Asante men's kente cloths from Ghana.

Contents

ACKNOWLEDGMENTS

I am grateful that Nancy E. Randolph of Just Write Books thought enough of my writing that she was willing to publish it. I learned everything I know about putting a book together from her. Her editing and advice were essential. I appreciated the fact that she was easy to work with, and I enjoyed doing this with her.

Most of my thanks must go to all the wonderful people that I interacted with in every country where I lived and visited. I am eternally grateful to all of them, even if I never learned their names. But there are those who I want to especially point out. They know who they are, even when I don't use their full names.

In the Philippines (1964-66): Ate, Kuya, Emma, Gigi, Leo, and Annie, Manung, Elmer, Father Postma, Wili, Sagangsan, Susan, Michael D., Mrs. Mateo, Danny, the nuns of Culion, all of my co-teachers, and Kevin Herbert who helped me remember parts of the Culion experience.

In Malaysia (1969-72): Sarasa and Bala, Noordin and Zakinah, Fred and June, Julie and Tom, Josephine, and Chin.

In Sri Lanka (1983-86): Indira, Chandra, Dinusha, and Chandeep, Lalith and Preethi, Heather and Sunita, Siri and Mrs. Fernando.

In Ghana (1990-97): Kwasi and Emma, Dramani, Evans, Kakra, John, Angie, Martha, Kwasi Patrick, Kojo, and Aiysha, Emmanuel, Edmond and Marian, Yemi, Serwaa, and the American Ambassador.

In Macedonia (2006): Danica and Petar, Mine and Jane, Fatma and Elez, Fatima, and Jasmine.

In all my travels: Milton Bennett, Gordon, Marj and Jim, Ruth and Harold, Wendy, Dick T., Michael M., the Samoan family, Fred and John, Raj, the Johanes family, Surander and Kajer, Dino, Renate, Mr. Yu, Mr. Li, Mr. Shen, and Miss Ling.

I will always cherish your friendship and opening up cultures to me, grateful that you were each a small part of my life.

My husband, Nate, knew nothing about my efforts to write a book, as I mentioned in my introduction. Still he has always been supportive of everything I have done, and I appreciate that more than he knows. My adult children, Windi and Sean, didn't know I was working on a book either. I trust that they won't be embarrassed about how I have portrayed their experiences living and traveling abroad. I hope they will be pleased with the result. And, finally, I hope my grandchildren will find their grandmother's life and travels in other cultures interesting enough to read as they grow older.

INTRODUCTION

I did not set out to write a book. It was only in 2012, during a writing workshop at Haystack Mountain School of Craft that I began writing. I didn't keep it up. Finally, a good friend invited me to join a local writing group. There I began writing random essays about some of my experiences as a Peace Corps Volunteer and subsequent life in other countries. Then, I began thinking I would write about my life abroad as a gift to my children and grandchildren. Years earlier, my grandfather Wilson had typed up a one-page history of his life for me. I treasured it. Anything else I knew about my family background came from births and deaths listed in an old Bible, some scraps of paper written by older relatives, and my research through Ancestry.com.

Before I ever began writing, I was fascinated with textiles. I began collecting them in the Philippines and during my long trip home that followed. In Malaysia three years later, I learned to make batik paintings. When I got back to the US I studied weaving and started creating wall pieces on a frame loom. By the time I returned from Sri Lanka, I was entering juried shows and taking on commissions. I mention this because textiles and my own fiber art pieces play a role in this book, as you will see.

About a year ago, a friend gave us a book he had written, and I noticed that he had used a Maine publishing company. I was curious and asked him about it. He gave me the contact information and urged me to speak to the publisher. When I did, she invited me to send her one of my essays. Then, if she thought I was promising, she would make an appointment with me to talk. I did and she did. That was the end of March, 2021.

I started writing essays with stories chronologically, trying to capture my experiences, along with my reflections and emotions, as I traveled my cross-cultural journeys. Sometimes I had a diary to refer to, but mostly I didn't. I just started writing, and, amazingly to me, my life began rolling out. One event, one person led to another. It didn't seem to require a plan. Of course, I failed to mention some things I later remembered, and had to return to include. Occasionally, I shared more than I wanted and had to reconsider. My writing wasn't always clear, too wordy, or contained too many passive 'to be' verbs. But, I felt for the first time that my efforts were going somewhere.

I was particularly interested in revealing the cross-cultural dynamics that were often missed or misunderstood in other cultures. I had previously taken some cross-cultural workshops at the Intercultural Communication Institute in Portland, Oregon, which is unfortunately now defunct. Those workshops and my own evolving experiences helped me recognize and analyze what I thought was going on in a new place. I tried to harvest those instances in my writing. Sometimes the examples were hilarious, others somewhat traumatic. In between there were occasions that were rather humorous, startling, maddening, and even beyond understanding, at least for me. Above all, I wanted to share what good fortune I felt for the many opportunities I experienced and enjoyed living in other cultures.

When I lived and traveled abroad in Asia and Africa I had never heard of "white privilege." This, I now know refers to the privilege that white people enjoy just by being white. Mostly, I think about it in reference to the United States with respect to African Americans in particular. I can see in retrospect, that my whiteness played a role abroad too, among people of color. I was visible and doors often opened for me. Being an American usually helped too. As much as I may have tried to downplay those factors, it is obvious to me now that my white privilege accompanied me almost everywhere.

What I have written is from the best of my memory. In the text, I use the old names of places and countries because that was true when I was there. When I have asked other individuals for help, I mentioned them in my acknowledgments. To get my facts and dates straight I occasionally did turn to Google, Wikipedia and other sources to confirm, clarify, or correct what I thought I remembered. I tried my best to be factual and truthful, but I doubt that I was entirely successful in that effort. My understandings, based on my own experiences and memory, were not always the whole truth, but often the truth from my somewhat limited perspective, a partial truth. I apologize for any mistakes or misunderstandings I might have made. None were intentional.

For an entire year I didn't tell my husband about a possible book. Nate knew I was writing, but only for my kids and grandchildren. He was writing too, so he asked no questions. Upon returning home from meeting with my publisher on March 31, 2022, I asked him to sit down as I had something to tell him. His first question was, "Did you get a job?" I responded with, "sort of." When I told him about the book he was obviously surprised, but happy for me. He couldn't believe I had kept my secret for a year. I hadn't told him because I didn't want him to be disappointed if it didn't work out. Luckily, neither of us was disappointed. I wanted to publish this book by my eightieth year—in that I will have been successful.

Susan W. Bowditch,
Friday, May 13, 2022

P. S. There are almost no photos of my life in the Philippines and my trip around the world. Those I show in the book were given to me by Peace Corps friends. My photos were all lost as I explain in the chapter on Malaysia.

STARTING UP

A red, single-engine propeller plane swooped down to pick us up. Piloted by Mr. O.C. Holt from Texas, the plane landed in my cattle rancher grandfather's pasture just outside of Atlanta, Kansas. My grandmother, mother, and I were flying to Canada. It was my first time in a plane.

I was four and my mother and I were headed to Winnipeg, Ontario in matching blue serge suits. I couldn't imagine why we were so dressed up. I remember that well because I got sick in flight, throwing up all over my new suit. When we stopped in Chicago to refuel, my mother removed my suit, put a coat on over my slip and took me to a department store in the city for some new clothes.

Back in the air, I managed to stay healthy until we landed in Winnipeg. There I vaguely remember going through stores of fine English bone china—my grandmother was a great collector. I had never seen so many dishes in my life, overwhelmed with lovely floral patterns in lively colors—cream pitchers and sugar bowls, dainty cups and saucers, elegant plates with matching bowls. This contrasted greatly with our final destination: my grandparents' fishing camp. Picked up by a hired hand in a car my grandparents kept in Ontario, we were eventually deposited in this remote location.

The cabin, rigged with barked logs, chinking that allowed daylight in, no electricity, a pump attached to a well outside, and inside mattresses atop platforms, spelled excitement to me. I loved that we were practically living outdoors; mice were checking out our food, squirrels snooped around the exterior of the cabin, and best of all, I was allowed to go outside to the bathroom.

My grandparents' cabin near Winnipeg, Ontario, Canada, where I stayed after my first flight in a small plane from my grandfather's pasture near Atlanta, Kansas, 1946.

My most vivid memory of that experience was floating in a fishing boat, foraging for fish down the middle of a beautiful long lake. An erratic electrical storm suddenly billowed up in the sky while we were still far from the cabin. My mother must have been scared to death because she, once again, removed all of my clothes to my slip, and told me to take off my shoes. My grandmother's hired man quickly engaged the motor, and we sped back down the lake. I only thought later that, in case the boat turned over in the storm, we would have had to swim. There was no mention, as I recall, of the imminent danger of death by lightning if we were in the water.

I had no idea what it would be like to live in another more distant country, nor would I find out for many years. Once in fourth grade, through the Weekly Reader, I discovered a story about a girl growing up in Samoa. The Samoan girl asked for pen pals and, for the first time, I decided to write to her. I was too naïve and hurt to grasp why she never responded. Only as an older student, did I begin to understand the host of other girls who would have wanted to be her pen pal. She must have been overwhelmed, but I never forgot her. I believe that reading about that Samoan girl was the beginning of my interest in traveling and living in foreign cultures.

By the time I was a teenager, we drove to California where I encountered the ocean for the first time. My birthday was in October, but long before I knew what a Scorpio was, I felt drawn to water. Later I worked summers in our town's public pool teaching swimming lessons, as a lifeguard and directing water ballet. On my bedroom wall, I hung the print of an artist's painting of the ocean. Seeing the ocean in person, though, was another thing. I was mesmerized with the wave action topped in white foam, the beautiful transparent color, and especially the limitless horizon. The only thing I could connect it to visually was the long perspective of acres and acres of wheat growing on my grandfather's farm in Kansas.

At sixteen, my next adventure was just across the border in Mexico, through Nogales, Arizona, to be exact. Mexico's border and people couldn't have been more different than Canada's—that was obvious. I loved the food—burritos, tacos, tamales. All of it tasted wonderful to my Midwestern palate, where most things were bland: meatloaf, cornbread, salad, green beans, and maybe apple pie for dessert. Here I could taste spices, a little heat, and strange mixtures of ingredients, all of which were new to me.

I think I enjoyed the open-air markets just as much. The stalls were so different from the shops on Poyntz Avenue in Manhattan, Kansas, where everything was labeled and categorized: Bettons' music store for records, Coles for clothes, Stevenson's for shoes, the drugstore for cherry cokes, Sears for ordering, and Woolworths for just about everything else. Here things were all mixed up, loud and colorful. I fell in love with the silver jewelry. I wish I could say I still had the gorgeous, embossed silver bracelet that wound around my wrist in a stylish way. It was stunning. My uncle helped me bargain for it—and what a bargain it was, even in 1957: five dollars.

In 1958, my parents traveled around the world on a mission for our government's aid program. As an agriculture economist, my dad became part of a fairly elite group chosen to advise on agricultural issues in several developing countries. This was interesting because my father, and most of the other professionals, had been from farm families. My mom went along for the ride, and we kids stayed home and worried during the month that they traveled. Everything changed when they returned from flying the old Pan Am flight trail that took them from Kansas City to Honolulu, from Bangkok to Jogjakarta, from Madras to New Delhi. Suddenly my mom was serving beef stroganoff (How did she get away with that?) to Hindu students and faculty at Kansas State College. We even had Indian brass bowls and cotton *sarees* on the table. Afterwards, I was encouraged to invite a variety of women college students to model their native traditional clothing at the high school for International Day.

My narrow world in the middle of the country was on a significant trajectory of change, even though I didn't know it yet. After college I would actually be living in another country, the first of several experiences of immersion in someone else's culture.

PEACE CORPS TRAINING IN HAWAII

I received my invitation to Peace Corps Training in mid-July, 1964. Thrilled that I was going to be in Hilo, Hawaii, training to teach in the Philippines, I was mentally ready to go. I accepted immediately and began my departure preparations. Having just graduated from college, I lived at home that summer. My mother and I sewed an outfit for me to wear on the plane, since dressing up to fly, in heels, was expected. I packed a few summer outfits, kissed my parents and my boyfriend, Dan, goodbye, and on August 31, off I went.

I had been a freshman in college when would-be President Kennedy announced his desire to create a Peace Corps for young people to learn about the world outside their frame of reference, to contribute something useful in a developing country, and to share that experience upon their return. Previously, I had considered teaching in a small one-room schoolhouse, like the one my father attended in Viola, Kansas. I had also considered becoming a missionary somewhere overseas. It seemed obvious that I was ready for a life-changing experience, and when the formation of the Peace Corps was announced it seemed to fit the bill. Most of my friends got married upon graduation or began graduate school. I stayed the course and joined the Peace Corps.

On the plane, I sat next to a beautiful dark-haired young woman in a white silk suit with a rose in her lapel. Her name was Sally, and she was also going to Hawaii for training. I discovered the six-hour flight to Honolulu from Los Angeles was full of new Peace Corps trainees—some for the Philippines, some for Malaysia, and the rest for Indonesia. I talked with several of them up and down the aisle as we flew. I met Gordon, who later became my boyfriend, despite his being assigned to Malaysia. It felt like we were all on track for a real adventure.

Outside of Hilo, part way up the extinct volcano of Mauna Loa, our training director met us at an old, abandoned school where we were to live together for the next three months. It was called Waiakea-uka. Soon we were assigned sleeping arrangements—one former classroom with bunk beds for the women, another for the men, and one room for the six married couples. We all wondered how that would work out, but the newlyweds were very creative. They strung shower curtains between their beds, cleaned out an old janitor's room, and traded off inhabiting that space on a rotating basis.

The challenging part for me was that the bathrooms were under the building, and the showers had only very cold water. Many braved that frigid water each morning, but I waited until after the physical education teacher had us run at the end of the training day. I was hot and sticky when I showered. Otherwise, we practiced a few hours daily with the language teachers. I learned Tagalog, while others learned Cebuano or Ilocano. The food was good because we had a local cook, so we only had to help clean up.

We were also supposed to contribute something to the Hilo community. In my case, a few women trainees and I formed a sewing group in which several local Japanese American ladies allowed us to pretend to teach them how to sew. It was a good experience. Later, after lengthy teacher training, we had an opportunity to help co-teach in a local elementary school. I had signed up for science, even though I was an art major in college. Somehow it sounded better than English or math, and I assumed my level was at least as high as a fifth grader's.

On other days, we were bussed to the former Hilo Hospital on Wainuenue Avenue, for the rest of our training, where the Malaysian and the Indonesian trainees were housed. There we got inoculations of gamma globulin, learned how to cut off a chicken's head—and did it. I enjoyed cross-cultural classes challenging us as to how to live in another culture. I even learned to pack a box with a web of string to assure the contents arrival across the ocean. We

Several of the women trainees in their individually sewn Filipina outfits preparing to welcome guests to the Peace Corps training site, Waiakea-Uka, Hilo, Hawaii, 1964. (l-r) Pat, Caroline, the author, Sydney, Bobbie Jean and Cathy.

were also interviewed by a psychiatrist to ascertain our emotional preparedness for the journey ahead. I loved every minute of it.

During training, my father phoned to let me know that he was being considered for a job at the University of Hawaii in Honolulu. He visited me after his interview there. Before I left for the Philippines, my father informed me that he had been offered and accepted the job. He was on his way home to help my mother prepare for the exciting, but long-distance move.

By November, if we hadn't been "de-selected"—a terrible name for those who were asked to leave—we headed to Honolulu for three days of Rest and Recreation (R and R) before leaving for Manila. Most of us had never traveled to Hawaii and I was happy to be assigned to a hotel somewhere near the famed Waikiki Beach. On the first day, I put my swimsuit on under my shorts and walked toward what I thought was the beach. I failed to ask directions and soon found myself heading toward an inland canal, the opposite of where I intended to go. I liked wandering around by myself once I straightened out my internal compass.

The night before we departed for the Philippines, I stopped in a restaurant. I ordered a hamburger and blueberry pie a la mode, a couple of favorites I wouldn't have again for two years. After walking around for a while again afterwards, I decided to stop in another restaurant and ordered the same thing, just to be on the safe side.

The next day we took flight over the blue expanse of the Pacific ocean, which was all we could see for hundreds of miles. We were nearly forty new Peace Corps Volunteers, one American staff person, and all the language teachers. During one stop in Guam to refuel, most of us ended up at the duty-free shop. Several of the Filipinos asked us to buy expensive items for them, like watches or radios, because we could bring them in duty-free and they couldn't. Fortunately, I didn't get involved in that.

The flight was more than twelve hours long, but we managed to walk up and down the aisle, drink cocktails, eat on a tray covered by a cloth napkin, laugh, and compare notes. We were nervous too. We had trained on a beautiful Hawaiian island, but it was not the Philippines. Someone told us that we would be able to smell garbage as we landed at the airport. I was not afraid because I thought I was ready for the big picture, but the details were still a question mark.

I don't remember smelling any garbage as we landed. As a matter of fact, I don't remember much of anything that first day, going through customs, getting on the bus to ride along the bay front to our hotel, or how I slept that inaugural night in Manila. I only remember going out into the stifling hot and humid air the next morning to find breakfast. A couple of us ended up in a bakery eating *ensaymadas* and drinking *calamansi* juice. Two new tastes—a great beginning.

Later, at the Peace Corps office I met my host family mother, along with her sister. A down-to-earth, lovely Filipino woman named Cenen, appeared very shy. I was to live with her family in Malolos, Bulacan, about forty kilometers from Manila. By comparison, her wealthy, well-traveled, sister spoke excellent English. I began to wish she were my host mother instead. But I was wrong. As it turned out, this family—Ate, Kuya, Emma, Leo, Gigi, and Annie—grew on me in wonderful ways. They changed the course of my life.

A mini-reunion of seven former Peace Corps Volunteers, group Philippines XIII, and spouses in Newport, Rhode Island, 2022. Covid was still active and we all tested before we met. This night was cold and we were forced to eat inside. (left to right) Jocie, April, Barbara, Katrina, the author, author's husband, Nate, Pat, Jerry, Bonnie, Doug, Bob, Norman, Kevin, and Joe.

The Philippines

My wonderful Filipino family whom I lived with in Malolos, Bulacan, as a Peace Corps Volunteer from 1964-66: Leo, Ate, Kuya, Annie, Emma, Gigi.

MALOLOS, BULACAN, THE PHILIPPINES

As a newly minted Peace Corps Volunteer, I had hoped to be stationed in the most southern island of Mindanao. I wanted as remote an assignment as possible, which for me, equaled a rugged experience. I should have guessed as I learned *Tagalog* that my assignment would be to the northern-most island of Luzon. And so, I found myself in the capital of the province just north of Manila: Malolos, Bulacan. It was a large town with a large central Catholic church, and many smaller *barrios* dividing the city. Malolos Pilot Elementary School was where I would co-teach fifth grade science. The nearby barrio of San Juan was where I would live with my host family. It was 1964.

Cenen and Jose were relatively well-off in the neighborhood. They had a painted cement house with a patio and a gate connected to a cement fence circling the property. Behind the house was the *bahay kubo*, the more common bamboo hut, where Manung, the older woman housekeeper, cooked our meals and where the four children slept. Emma, the eldest, was already in high school when I arrived. Leo was next, a twelve-year-old, the only boy. Gigi, aged ten, and Annie, aged five, followed him. As one of her teachers, I got to know Gigi the best. With her sparkling black eyes and a wide smile, I thought she was special.

Kuya (Jose) was a city engineer who commuted to Manila daily in his renovated WWII American jeep. *Ate* (Cenen) was a teacher in my school. Their two professional incomes helped explain their comfortable home. It was furnished with modern furniture covered in plastic. It also boasted a TV set. I certainly didn't expect to live in such a home as a Peace Corps Volunteer. But I was grateful for my own small room, which had a built-in closet and dressing table. I slept on a caned bed which allowed air to flow through. I was content.

I loved my fifth-grade co-teachers. During breaks they would make *champorado* from the cocoa and rice in boxes marked as a gift from the United States to the Philippines. I am pretty sure it was meant for the school children and poorer people in the barrios. But I decided not to make a fuss. I also have to admit that I joined in—*champorado* was delicious.

I tried to work with teachers in the inductive, rather than the deductive, method of teaching elementary science. There were plenty of teachers in the Philippines. Still the methods were at least sixty years old, a result of the American colonization of the country, following that of the Spaniards. Lots of Tagalog words were actually Spanish words. However, for more than a half century, children were taught in English from the third grade on, so most everyone who was educated could speak fairly fluent English.

Whenever I entered the classroom, the students whooped and hollered. After a few times, once they were quiet, I asked them why they did that with me and not the other teachers. There was a silent pause and then one of the students volunteered: "Because you are sexy!" I couldn't have been more surprised, though a little flattered too. I am not sure they knew what the word "sexy" meant, but at least I had their attention.

The principal was another issue. I wore the uniform faithfully—white blouse and blue *ramie* skirt—and tried to follow all the rules she put in motion. But one thing kept bothering me. When any of the students made drawings or paintings she critiqued them by writing across the artwork. I couldn't stand that and finally wrote her a letter complaining about the disrespect displayed to the students by her actions. For some reason, I can't remember whether she responded or not. Luckily, I didn't get fired or reported to the Peace Corps Office.

After a few months, I decided that I would like to see what the other schools in our district were doing in science and whether I could help out. So, I got the list and set out to find out during the times I wasn't teaching. I wrote letters to the principals and later met with the teachers about what I was doing in Malolos. Many complained that I was an expert, and they couldn't follow it. I retorted I was no expert, as my background was in art, but I was trained in this method of teaching science. In other words, if I could do it, so could they.

I loved traveling around and meeting teachers from every school. But my favorite school was on Pamarawan island. To get there, I had to take a *banca* to which the driver had attached a motor. Within a half-hour on a river, we had reached this island on Manila Bay. All of the houses were on stilts because at high tide the land was flooded. I had been warned to time my arrival accordingly. Luckily, the tide was low when I arrived the first time, but that meant walking through deep mud to get to the school. The principal, Mrs. Trinidad Mateo, greeted me, a wise and beautiful, earthy older woman. I grew to love her, sometimes had meals with her family in their home, once sleeping on their floor because I couldn't get back to Malolos before high tide.

I had many fascinating experiences in the Philippines. I encountered only kindness and warmth. At one point, I was asked to be *Reyna Elena*, as part of the Flora de Mayo festival. A beautiful green and white satin traditional evening gown was created for me with the big sleeves that harked back to the elite Spanish women's gowns. Someone put my hair up into a chignon, and I rode around Malolos in a convertible with my friend Pol, a handsome, rather tall Filipino man, sitting beside me. I felt like a queen, waving my hand to the gathered crowds.

My Filipino family introduced me to lots of local food. For breakfast, Manung always scrambled eggs and bought fresh *pan de sal* from the local bakery. I was addicted. For lunch we often had *pancit*, noodles sautéed with vegetables and maybe some pork wrapped in a newspaper that you could pick up on the street. *Lumpia*, the thin transparent wrap of chopped palm heart, nuts, and veggies, was wonderful. I loved *adobo manok* created by a subtle marinade of chicken, garlic, ginger, soy sauce, and vinegar, with a bay leaf tucked in, cooked till the liquid was gone. Coconut milk was often added. For Christmas Eve, the family baked a complete fish with all the trimmings. Dessert was surprising to me: a can of fruit cocktail mixed with sweetened condensed milk and frozen. The one thing I never tried, only heard about, was *balut*, a fertilized duck egg. I just couldn't stomach it, but it was considered a true delicacy.

When it was time for me to leave the Philippines, there were several 'Blow Outs' in my honor, which meant a party with lots of food and small gifts. The most memorable party was in one of the district schools. After the food and drink had been circulated, the teachers presented me with a framed carving of a woman in traditional dress, signed on the back by all of them. I was grateful and gave a short speech of thanks, confirming the pleasure it had been to work with the science teachers there. The surprise came at the end: they officially asked if I would send them a new television for their school once I returned to the US. I was flabbergasted at this request and made polite excuses, including the fact that I didn't even own a TV myself.

The Philippines was a great first overseas learning experience, and a treasured one. Still there were some things I was not fond of. I disliked the fact that many Filipino women grabbed my purse, or the tag at the neck of my blouse, and asked if it was an American brand name. Sometimes I felt there was almost too much pro-American sentiment since World War II, although that was beginning to change among students at the university. Still, conversely, the old Spanish custom of single women being chaperoned around single men, stood strong. A man was never to be alone with me, because, if seen, he might be forced to marry me. Nevertheless, married men often tried to touch me or hold my hand, like Mr. G., during a dance performance at a school festival. Unlike for single men and women, there seemed to be no consequences to married men making advances to other women.

Fortunately, my Filipino family stood up for me when the neighbors questioned my independent behavior. I had explained that American women often traveled safely on their own. There was always a kind of wavy cross-cultural line that I had to navigate between what was expected of me as a young woman in the Philippines, and what was important to me personally. It was a lesson I tried to apply to every subsequent overseas living situation I was fortunate enough to experience.

THE LEPER COLONY

For my first summer project as a Peace Corps Volunteer in the Philippines, I chose to work with children of lepers on the small island of Culion, situated just north of the much bigger island of Palawan. I could have chosen professional summer workshops for teaching science instead, but that sounded more like work. I wanted to do something more interesting, unfamiliar to me, out of my comfort zone.

Getting there took a couple of days. First, I bumped along on a bus from Malolos to Manila. There I met three other PCVs, Tom, Kevin and Dianne. Together we took another bus south to Batangas. Then it was an overnight boat trip to the island of Coron, followed by a smaller boat to Culion Island. There were cots on the deck of the first boat where we could sleep overnight, but mostly we stayed awake talking quietly and imagining the unusual destination to which we were headed.

When morning arrived, our small boat docked on the water facing the only town on Culion. We were met by a Catholic nun who led us to our housing, a square building with rented rooms in the town's center. After dropping our bags, we were taken up to the convent to meet the children. They were excited to see us. I was happy that they all seemed perfectly normal. I am not sure what I expected. I really knew nothing about leprosy and hadn't ever met someone with the disease. Later I would get that opportunity.

Leprosy, I learned, was a terrible disease, with an even greater stigma. The nuns told us that those with leprosy often lost fingers or toes over time. Unfortunately, so-called "lepers" were separated early from their children or other family members who were free of leprosy. Most of the time they had to look at their youngsters through a glass window. The lepers lived together in a kind of hospital compound, or leprosarium. Family members were allowed to visit occasionally, but constant contact over time could lead to developing leprosy. It was very hard for married couples, but just as difficult for children of lepers, who essentially became orphans at birth. At the time, I believed Culion was the only place in the Philippines that housed victims of leprosy. Later, I learned there had been another leprosarium on Cebu island.

Meanwhile, back at the convent, and on a lighter note, the nuns served us cold Cokes with fresh homemade donuts. I couldn't believe donuts. I hadn't had one in over a year. What a treat. We talked about what our work would be. Because I could sew, I was assigned to work with the older girls in making their school uniforms, white blouses with blue skirts. I thought I could handle that.

I went to the convent every day after school to sew. As for skirts, once the length and waist for each girl was determined, I could just gather the fabric, sew it to a waist band and hem the skirt. That was easy. As for blouses, since I didn't have a pattern, I just drew an outline of each of the girl's current blouse onto a piece of butcher paper. If the girl had grown or their shape had changed, I tried to adapt it. But the results were pretty close to disaster. I had never created blouses without patterns. Sleeves pulled at too small armholes and darts were often in the wrong places. I don't even remember how I put in buttonholes or snaps. But the girls helped me sew them and they wore them anyway.

Life on Culion was pretty slow, as several dozen families lived outside the leprosarium and nun's compound, ran businesses, taught in the school, or did other basic jobs. There was even special Culion money, used primarily in the leprosarium. To have some fun we invited other young people to join us in the living room of our house, put music on the radio and danced on weekends. That was how I got to know Danny.

He and I spent some free time together, though he was at least four years younger than I. I was twenty-two and he was probably eighteen. I met his family and he showed me around Culion island, including a trip up a river on a *banca*. The old-fashioned

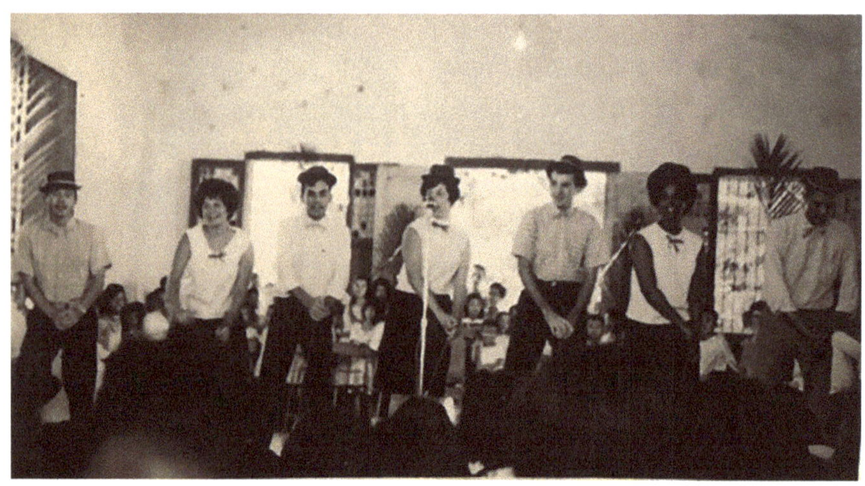

A performance by several Peace Corps Volunteers, working with the children of parents with leprosy, to entertain them, in the leprosarium, Culion, Palawan, Philippines, 1965.

idea of a young unmarried woman needing to be chaperoned when with a young man, I allowed to fly out the window. Was it because we were on a remote island, that it didn't seem necessary to comply? Even though nothing untoward happened, I was clearly not being culturally sensitive. Probably the neighborhood was talking about me. Danny knew about my boyfriend, Gordon, in Malaysia. Still, according to my Peace Corps colleague, Tom, it looked like I was carrying a mattress on my back every time I went out with him.

Occasionally, our group of PCVs got together to entertain the men and women in the leprosy compound. We put on short musical performances, singing songs together and individually. At one point, it seemed we couldn't remember all the words of a particular song and ended up laughing at ourselves on stage. If I remember correctly, our audience laughed too. Individually, we sang songs we knew we could get through. Since I was from Kansas I chose "Home on the Range" and "I was born in Kansas". Our efforts were received with pleasure. Applause often came from those who no longer had fingers, using their stumps instead. We were all extremely humbled by this response, admiring the courage and bright spirits of those who suffered from such disabilities. We hoped we might have made a small difference in their daily lives, plus we had a good time too.

It was hard to leave this isolated island and its people—including all those tethered to the leprosy hospital and compound, those who worked in the town, the nuns in the convent, and especially the children who had been left behind. But, after two months, it was time for me to return to my teaching job in Malolos.

THE CIRCLE TOUR

Skimming just barely above tall buildings, my Philippine Airlines flight appeared to dive for the sea, instead of Kai Tak Airport. Soon after that scary landing, I stepped onto solid ground. On my first trip abroad by myself, I had alighted in Kowloon, Hong Kong, about to begin "The Circle Tour" around Southeast Asia. I felt adventurous and very adult.

The Philippines had been my first experience of living outside the U.S. But flying there became one of many flights overseas. And—while trips like this would never replace the fullness and engagement I captured by actually living abroad—I enjoyed many fun dips into other cultures. This was going to be one of them.

I had saved up five hundred US dollars for this trip, from the seven hundred and twenty dollars I had earned the year before as a Peace Corps Volunteer. It was Christmas and I hadn't imagined how cold it was going to be here—nor the city's congestion and intimidating skyscrapers. With a drop of nearly forty degrees Fahrenheit from Manila, the cold insisted the first thing I did was buy a thick mohair sweater for the duration.

My then boyfriend, Gordon, now a Peace Corps Volunteer in Malaysia, joined me in Hong Kong too. We hadn't seen each other in over a year, and we soon realized that we didn't know each other well, despite dating during Peace Corps training. But we had fun, sitting in the lobbies of expensive hotels just sipping coffee and watching people, climbing to the top of Victoria Peak opposite Kowloon, and searching for gifts to give each other for Christmas. I spent fifty US dollars on an ivory and ebony chess set for him and indulged myself in a cocktail dress with a flowing coat, created from a magenta and silver Indian silk *saree*. It had cost another fifty dollars. This sum was greater than I had ever spent for an item of clothing. Ever.

Our next stop on The Circle Tour was Bangkok. I had family friends working for USAID there. We called Harold and Ruth with no advance notice, practically showing up on their doorstep. They kindly took us in, but I realized I should have written first. Not very adult. Apart from the busy traffic and congestion around Sukhumvit Road, Bangkok seemed amazing to me: the delicate Thai architecture of the temples, delicious fresh food, lovely looking women in sarongs, and such gorgeous silk fabrics. Being a fabric person, I was very taken with Thai silk. I thought it to be indigenous, but I found out later that much of the silk industry had been enlarged and refined for western use by a man named Jim Thompson.

The site of the Temple of the Emerald Buddha, Bangkok, Thailand, with the interesting and delicate symbols on the temple roofs, intended to keep the bad spirits away, 1986.

Thompson, an American, somehow involved in WWII, perhaps as a spy, fell in love with Thailand. In his fabrics, he created unusual hues by combining different colors of silk for the weft and the warp. That gave the silk a stunning shimmering look, which changed colors from different viewing angles. I loved it and bought a few pieces to take home.

Kuala Lumpur, Malaysia, was next and the choice of Indian, Malay, Chinese and European cuisine signaled an astonishing mix of cultures. Despite that, I still stuck with the more familiar Chinese and western food. But, while there, I was thrilled to experience something that was new to me: the hand stamped *batik* fabrics. A hot wax resist, used to separate different dyes on the cotton cloth, created an effect that was modern and charming. Batik artists had begun to make the art scene too, giving rise to fabulous paintings and wall pieces. I was quite struck by the unusual use of a fabric technique to make interesting art. Unfortunately, on my Volunteer salary, I couldn't afford to buy these, but bought fabric lengths instead. I also enjoyed watching the women along Batu Road, in their separate cultural outfits: Indians in silk sarees with gold trim, Malays in bright *kain* batik, and Chinese in satiny silk *cheongsams*. Meanwhile, we rode around in *trishaws* and mostly ate Chinese street food. Once Gordon and I took the elevator to the top of the Federal Hotel for Steak Diane and dancing, a real American treat.

Singapore was just a short flight away. It had only recently broken away from the new country of Malaysia, which included Malaya, Sabah and Sarawak, but now, no longer Singapore. Lee Kuan Yew, the president of Singapore, had very strict policies with respect to both foreigners and his own people. By the late 1960s, long hair on men was prohibited and short skirts on women were frowned upon. But the city was thriving economically, and growing, with tall buildings beginning to stud the landscape.

We walked down to the docks to see what was going on. There weren't as many freighter ships as we would have thought, and cruise ships weren't yet visible either. As a city state and an island nation without any natural resources, it needed the outside world to survive. At the time we visited the city had made it through riots between the

Chinese and Malays. But it seemed obvious, given its position in the South China Sea, that Singapore was going to have a great future.

The last stop was Sabah, Malaysia, on the Borneo island that was half Malaysian and half Indonesian. Gordon was teaching here, in the town of Beaufort, which he described as populated mostly by Chinese. Instead of going there, we traveled up country to visit an open-air market among the Kadazan people. Impressed by the variety of hats on their heads and back-baskets on their backs, I found the women's traditional dress particularly interesting. They each wore a tight fitting black handwoven cotton sarong with a single red stripe circling it, just below the hips. When they walked, the stripe moved with them in a sort of flirtatious way.

We also poked around Jesselton, Sabah's capital city and a small port. It was here that I finally tried real Malay curries for the first time. The spark of spice and heat jolted me initially, but the long smooth finish of the coconut cream captured me. I was hooked. The combination was almost life changing. It was as though I had been waiting for a curry to happen to me. Somehow, despite its "exotic" origins, it suited me perfectly.

After a few days, Gordon and I said our goodbyes, and I flew back to Manila, my teaching job in Malolos, and my life with Ate, Kuya and the kids. There were no more curries for me again until my trip home.

THE MANGYANS

After stepping onto the sizzling tarmac following our short flight to the island, I was relieved to book a jeep taxi and get on our way. In fact, I congratulated myself on how quickly I'd adapted to being back in the Philippines, even though I had never traveled by taxi here before. Still, there were four of us and I knew we would be more comfortable than in a bus. Of course, that bubble burst when more people joined us, several hanging onto the sides of the jeep, while I took ten-year-old Sean on my lap in front, and Nate squeezed fifteen-year-old Windi in beside him. The heat from the thin floor of the vehicle was almost more than I could bear—

thank goodness I had on sneakers instead of flip flops. We braced ourselves for what I knew would be a wild ride of more than five hours over a steep rocky trail around the edge of the mountains, from Occidental Mindoro to Oriental Mindoro. If the scenery was beautiful, I hardly noticed, so focused was I on making sure we made it safely to Mansalay.

I asked to be taken to the Catholic Father's house. Shortly after we arrived, I could hardly believe my eyes when Wili walked in. She had been told by Father Postma that a friend was coming, but not who. After twenty years we recognized each other—graying hair and all—and we hugged, exclaiming our mutual surprise in a happy mix of Mangyan, Tagalog and English. She told my family in Tagalog that we used to share a blanket together, meaning we were close. I couldn't believe I understood. Soon, Father Postma joined us, almost as young and lively as before, wearing a beaded Mangyan necklace and bracelets, in a chartreuse tee shirt and flowered Bermuda shorts. After I introduced my family to him, he suggested we take off for Panatayan village before it started to rain, and that everyone was waiting for us there.

We hopped into his great old Land Rover, a welcome relief from our overcrowded jeep taxi, and drove down into a dry riverbed. This was an itinerary I had never taken before and didn't even know that it was possible. Rather than the nearly three hours it had taken me to walk up the path into Hananoo Mangyan territory previously, we were going to be driven part-way on the hard, flat dirt. Our goal was the bottom backside of a steep mountain upon which Panatayan sat. For everyone but me that meant about a thirty-minute hike, as the kids and Nate scampered to the top with Father Postma. Wili stayed behind with me. "*Dahan, dahan*" we climbed, slowly in the rain together. I didn't do straight up very fast, and it was nearly an hour before we reached the top. But I paused midway to rest and enjoyed the view of the riverbed below, the dense tropical greenery around me, the fuzzy blue mountains in the background, and, most of all, the waiting faces hanging over the ledge at the top. I was happily soaked when we finally emerged.

I came to this small mountain village of Panatayan in 1966 as a

Peace Corps Volunteer. It was near the end of my two years of service, the last summer following my teaching career in Malolos that I heard about a project to work with an ethnic group up in the mountains of Oriental Mindoro. The Hananoo Mangyans had been on Oriental Mindoro island since about nine hundred AD. The settlement was so remote that they had their own language and writing system and had not been influenced by the occupancy of the Spaniards, nor later by that of the Americans. Legend had it that they may have been among the first in the islands to trade with the Chinese. They barely had anything to do with the lowland Filipinos, at least until recently. The project was focused on helping the Mangyans to become more literate in Tagalog. The reason was clear: the lowland Filipinos had started to move into Mangyan territory and take control of their land where they cultivated dry rice in a slash and burn manner. Just before I arrived, Wili and her husband Sagangsan, had lost two of their children in a drowning incident perpetrated by a group of lowland Filipinos. The Mangyan children were visiting the beach near Mansalay. These tragic circumstances alone were enough to motivate me to join the project.

Of course, I was still pretty naive. Even though I had been a PCV for nearly two years in Malolos I had lived with a relatively well-off Filipino family. So, this project captivated me. I joined a group of four male PCVs, as no other females had expressed interest. We traveled together by bus through the island of Luzon, then an overnight ferry, a filthy hotel in Calapan City, and another bus ride until we finally made it to Mansalay. There we were met by the Catholic priest, Father Postma, for orientation to life among the Mangyans. We had been told to bring only things we could carry on our backs as we trekked into the mountains.

I had never backpacked in my life and had no idea how to begin. So, I put something together with a few clothes, some books, and an easel. I covered all of this with a piece of canvas I had saved for oil painting, then tied the whole thing together with a rope. It was an awkward pile of my material assets if ever there was one. In the end–with suppressed laughter I am sure–the bundle was redone and carried up the mountain by one of the young Mangyan men who

The nipa hut, surrounded by bougainvillea flowers, where the author and her family resided during their visit to her Mangyan friends in Pana-tayan, Philippines, 1986.

would lead me to Panatayan. Incredibly in retrospect, I followed, climbing in a sundress and sandals. After nearly three hours I met Wili, her husband, Sagangsan, and their surviving children. I moved into the little nipa house right next to hers, displacing another PCV named Michael, who moved to another Mangyan village so I could live here.

Almost exactly twenty years later, I could never have predicted that my children and husband would join me in returning to this place. And, yet, on this day we were here. It was Nate who had said to me before we left our home in Sri Lanka: "Well, we can all walk—let's go visit the Mangyans!" But it was my daughter who, not so compassionately, retorted: "I sure hope this is worth it to someone besides Mom."

Now that we were unpacking in our own very lovely little "*bahay kubo,*" a nipa thatched roof wooden hut, with sleeping platforms on each wall, and bougainvillea flowers cascading outside the glassless windows, even Windi could see the rustic charm of it. But it was the people that I had learned to admire and love here that mattered most

The author talking and taking notes with her Mangyan friend, Wili, in Father Postma's hut, Panatayan, Philippines, 1986.

to me. Those who knew me as a Tagalog teacher of sorts, had been waiting at the top of that escarpment. They were kind enough to re-introduce themselves as I approached and greeted each one. Young students before, now most were mothers and fathers. Introductions were casual and warm: babies at the breast of some, there was Unmong, Bukas, Epang, Paulo, Tio and Maming, who would later cook our supper. It was almost too much to take in for one evening. After eating, in the early darkness of the tropics we took our leave for much needed sleep following an eventful day. Wili brought a lit candle and crouched just outside our hut to talk quietly with me in my broken and all-but-forgotten Mangyan and Tagalog before we slept. And sleep we did, as if we had never slept before.

The landscape was dramatically changed: many new plantings, new little homes, even a small new school. In my previous life here, I had tried to help students learn Tagalog, even though I wasn't totally fluent. In the process I learned some Mangyan. Their script was completely new to me. Each figure represented a consonant, with an extra mark that showed which vowel followed. Understanding the meaning depended on the context. I loved the fact that the Mangyans still wrote poetry called *ambahans*. A hollow bamboo rod with many ambahans on it, had been created for me and given to me as a gift on my departure in 1966.

I remembered how slow and pleasant life was here. I loved the unhusked rice cooked daily as the staple, but which lowland Filipinos fed to their dogs. The rice, paired with cooked leaves or root vegetables constituted their daily diet, sometimes with a tin of fish from town. This is what Father Postma had asked me to bring to the Mangyans initially: tins of tuna or marinated herring. I once tried to introduce pancakes over an open fire but wasn't as successful as I had hoped. On another day I found myself literally thirsting for a Pepsi and walked all the way down the mountain and back in one day for that treat alone. I also tried chewing betel nut for the first time. The nut, wrapped in betel pepper leaves with a little lime, was a mild stimulant. But it caused a red liquid to drip from the side of your mouth, so not a pretty sight on me.

Of course, all of life was not easy on Panatayan. Diseases and illnesses were sometimes fatal with no readily available medical treatment. I had occasionally been asked to lance a boil or clean a

Father Antoon Postma who worked with the Mangyan people until his death in Panatayan, Oriental Mindoro, Philippines, 1986. He had left the priesthood, married a Mangyan woman, and they had several children together.

The author with her daughter, Windi, and Wili, wiht her daughter, Su-san, the author's namesake among the Mangyans, 1986.

wound and apply antibiotic cream. Sanitary facilities were basically nil. While I enjoyed bathing in the little waterfall below the nearby stream, it was not fun chasing off wild pigs every time I "went to the bathroom" up in the field. Finally, I remembered Father Postma asking me if I had had any experience delivering babies because Wili was pregnant when I arrived. I hadn't but agreed I would help if asked. Halfway into my time there Wili delivered a little girl with Sagangsan's help, as she crouched in the middle of the night below her hut. I found out when I awoke the next morning, surprised and delighted to meet my new namesake: Susan.

Twenty years later, we visited Sagangsan who lay in a hammock in an open pavilion, unable to move. The sight of this once virile and strong gentle man saddened me greatly. He could barely talk, but I tried, knowing that he would probably not last the year. I also hugged their daughter, Susan, a matter of great joy to me. Now twenty years old, she had just gotten married. I gave her a pair of silver earrings to match the ones I bought for myself in Manila. I imagined us sometime in the future, wearing our earrings together, but across the world.

The other thing I wanted to remember was watching both Windi and Sean play basketball on the dirt court in the center of the village. My kids were in shorts and tee shirts, but some of the boys they were playing with were in G-strings. I took a photo of this sparkling cross-cultural moment when it didn't matter who you were, or where you came from.

Our visit was soon coming to an end, and I dreaded the sorrow that I would experience departing, once again. The last time I left I felt sure I would never return. Wili had given me an old antique Chinese honey jar that she had found in the mountains, a remnant of an ancient trading past. In return I gave her a small silver and turquoise Navajo pin that my grandmother had given me. And I cried all the way down the mountain.

Before leaving this time, I encountered Paulo, who invited me to come sit with him as he cooked his mid-day meal over an open fire pit. He was still tall and handsome, but for some reason had never married. I sat with him quietly for a while, before I spoke to him in Tagalog: "*Sana, babalik ulit ako dito.*" Hopefully, I will return here. His reply showed his wisdom beyond mine: "*Masyado kang tatanda.*" You will be too old.

On our final day a church service led by Father Postma, announced to me that it was Sunday. I learned he was living

Our son, Sean, playing basketball with Mangyan children, Panatayan, Oriental Mindoro, Philippines, 1986.

A Mangyan man wearing a traditional g-string, and embroidered shirt in red stitched Mangyan symbols meant to ward off evil, in Panatayan, the Philippines, 1986.

in Panatayan full time. He strolled to the altar in his flowered shorts, plus a dark blue frock, decorated with Mangyan symbols sewn in red stitches across its surface. Many men wore their culturally symbolic shirts. The women dressed in their own handwoven *ramit,* the indigo sarongs. I had purchased two of them already and offered more than the few dollars the women asked. This only confused them. Instead, they handed us gifts that gradually filled our plastic bags: baskets, beaded necklaces and bracelets, embroidered shirts, and new ambahans on bamboo. We were feeling rich with gratefulness for these kind people, their generosity, love and respect. We hoped they felt our love and respect in return.

During the service, and because I was a coward, I decided to take my leave ahead of Nate and the kids. I couldn't stand to say good bye one more time, one final time. And so I walked out slowly, stood at the back of the little bamboo church, took one last look at these people who had welcomed my return with my family, and headed back down the mountain, to the Land Rover waiting in the still dry creek bed, sobbing all the way.

Flying Around the World

The author tossing coins into the Trevi Fountain in Rome for good luck.

MANILA TO KUALA LUMPUR VIA SABAH

Thirty-three Filipino co-teachers and friends, plus my Filipino family—Kuya, Ate, Emma, Leo, Gigi and Annie—gathered on the runway at Manila airport to wish me farewell. It felt like a magical moment initially, but then switched to a sorrowful one. Magical, in that I was very touched that so many Filipino friends came to see me off, and sorrowful, because I wasn't sure whether I would see any of them again. Just twenty-three years old on July 18, 1966, I was mourning.

My parents were on the plane already, watching me say goodbye. They had come to visit me at the close of my Peace Corps sojourn, joining me for my last week there, together with my Filipino family. Finally, I climbed aboard the plane and sat with them, unable to speak. On my father's lap was the ancient Chinese honey jar, given to me by my Mangyan friend, Wili, before I walked away from her over the mountains. My experience working with the Mangyans that summer had been very special. The old jar was one among many that had been discovered, off and on, buried around Mangyan territory. This one was very big, but fragile.

Now, as I tried to gather myself together, we were already en route to Borneo. Flying over Palawan, my father talked briefly about his time there during WWII. But on this day, he was on some university expedition, joining his University of Hawaii colleague, Dr. Hendrickson, to meet local farmers in Sabah. I was meeting my then Peace Corps/Malaysian boyfriend, Gordon. Within a couple of hours we were in Sabah. By then, I was able to hug him and greet Dr. Hendrickson. We spent some time in Jesselton, eating

Chinese food for lunch at a street stall, and in my case, using chop sticks for the first time. I was starting to recover.

Soon we were headed up to Kundasang, Gordon's new site. It was a couple of hours in an old Land Rover with flat leather seats against metal, bouncing up and down on even older roads. But we were also climbing higher, and it was getting cooler as we left the heat of the coast behind. The sight of Mount Kinabalu was breathtaking. The next day we walked up as far as we could, my mother wearing only flip flops, which she soon had to abandon to bare feet, walking in cold mud. I raced Gordon up the mountain as far as I could and still breathe.

The next few days were a mix of Sabah highlands and the kind of food my mother would make in the fall-like weather at home. She cooked everything from roast beef to pork chops and hamburger, with mashed potatoes and French fries, to succotash, green beans, corn on the cob and omelets, along with cooked rhubarb and vanilla pudding for dessert. I had no idea where we got all those ingredients. I hadn't eaten real heartland American food in nearly two years.

Meanwhile, my father and his colleague visited with Malaysians and agricultural Peace Corps Volunteers in the area, impressed that Americans with only a liberal arts education could do so much. These particular Volunteers were clearing land, planting it, and building small homes, not for themselves, but for the Dusun people of the area.

After a few days, my parents and Dr. Hendrickson took off for Kuala Lumpur, Malaysia. I caught up writing letters, one in Tagalog to the Mangyans, while Gordon applied to the Economics Department at the University of Hawaii in Honolulu, for a master's degree program. Together we played chess and enjoyed chrysanthemum tea, with popcorn my mother had left behind.

After a couple of days I departed, to continue my journey of several months—the long way around—to my new home in Honolulu. I had asked my father to loan me the equivalent of my readjustment allowance, around one thousand US dollars, for travel. While it was meant to be used to help Returned Peace Corps Volunteers (RPCVs) to settle into life in the U.S., this loan gave me the opportunity to see more of the world first. When I returned home and got a job, I would pay him back.

After sorting out my ticket at Cathay Pacific in Jesselton, I got on the next flight, enjoying chicken curry and bird's nest soup for lunch. This was back in the day when the meals in flight were delicious, reflecting local cuisine, and served with real spoons, knives and forks. At the stopover in Singapore, I ran into Mal, one of the guys who had worked with the Mangyans when I was there. Together we shared some *sate* meat on sticks with rice cakes in woven strips of banana leaf. He was headed to Indonesia and I to the Malay peninsula. When I arrived in Kuala Lumpur (KL) my parents were still there, staying in the fancy Merlin Hotel. My father was in work mode, my mother in shopping mode. Into connecting with other Volunteers, I took off for the Peace Corps hostel.

At the hostel, there were many former Volunteers staying from all over, but mostly from the Philippines. Michael, who had given me the use of his house among the Mangyans, turned up too. My parents invited the two of us over for *crêpes suzette*—of all things—in the hotel restaurant. Afterwards we joined a party at the hostel who were happily eating durian. Durian was a tropical fruit so stinky I couldn't even allow myself to try it. It had been described to me as "old cheese and garlic drained through an old soldier's sock." I had juicy mangosteens instead.

My parents soon took off for Bangkok, my passport in hand, to secure a visa for me to travel to Indonesia. Because of the recent Confrontation between Malaysia and Indonesia, I couldn't get the visa in KL. In the meantime, I spent my time looking at batik fabrics, as well as lovely batik paintings by Chuah Thean Teng and Seah Kim Joo, which I still couldn't afford, walking among the few galleries on Batu Road.

One night Michael called the hostel asking for me to come to the Peace Corps director's home for a get together. He had brought tapes of Mangyan music to share with other Volunteers, as well as a letter and photo from Wili for me. I was excited to be reconnected to her so soon. Michael and I subsequently spent some time wandering around KL, swimming at Weld Pool, eating ice cream cones, enjoying Chinese street food, and just experiencing being in another country. Frankly, like other former Volunteers, I needed a break, some time to relax, recover, and regroup after my life in the Philippines. I wasn't reflecting much yet, but that would come. It was all good.

Meanwhile, Dr. Hendrickson was still in KL and asked if I wanted to travel to see the giant sea turtles laying their eggs on the Malayan east coast. I asked Michael if he wanted to go along too, but he said it sounded boring. Besides he was meeting a friend from New York in Bangkok soon, so we parted ways.

Instead, I took the trip to the east coast to spend most of the night in an old colonial Government Rest House near Dungun. Dr. Hendrickson knocked on my door at midnight, so I got dressed and joined him at the beach waiting for the turtles. I was soon amazed to see these giant animals lumbering slowly out of the water and crawling up the sand. Their breathing was loud and labored. About six feet long, they weighed between 700 and 1,000 pounds each. Soon, they dug nests in the sand and dropped hundreds of eggs which looked like ping pong balls. Afterwards they covered the nests to let the eggs mature and then slid back down into the ocean.

At 3:30am I went back to bed until 6 am, when I got up at another knock on the door. After a breakfast of cold eggs and hard toast, British style, and fresh orange juice, Malaysian style, we headed back to KL. In a Mercedes Benz taxi, we rode through the beautiful, green and lush jungle over the mountains, stopping only once for the famous sweet and sour pork at the little town of Bentong.

Spending a few days more with my PCV friends, I lunched at the A & W Root Beer shop near the American Embassy, saw the latest movie, *Mary Poppins*, and enjoyed dinner and dancing at the top of the Federal Hotel, once again. Some Volunteers who had been to Saigon reported that the USAID people lived as if there were no war going on thirty kilometers away. Holed up behind sandbags, Saigon had a midnight curfew, and the petty fighting going on among US agencies to win the war was barely concealed. I was beginning to get bored and restless. Walking back to the hostel one night, a young Malaysian man on a bicycle reached out and grabbed my breast, cycling away as I nearly fell into a small canal. It was time to go.

KUALA LUMPUR TO BANGKOK VIA BALI

I took off at sunset for the one-hour, twenty-minute flight to Jakarta. Someone at the airport gave me Indonesian rupiahs for dollars on the black market. That night I stayed at the upscale Hotel Indonesia—way out of my class because it cost eleven US dollars. That would be my most expensive overnight for a long while. But I enjoyed an American-style hamburger dinner that evening in the Java Room, which, for me, seemed an oxymoron.

I got up at four-thirty in the morning to take a taxi to the airport for my flight to Bali. As the only white person waiting in the mob at the airport, I understood that there hadn't been many tourists in the last few years. For the first time I felt a little vulnerable, traveling alone in a country where I'd never been. But when I got on the plane, a French couple was sitting right across the aisle. It turned out that they spoke no English, some Bahasa Indonesian, and, of course, French. I knew a little French, a little Malay, and, of course, English. We did our best to communicate as we ate our breakfast in flight: meat and rice wrapped in an egg omelet and a banana coated in green gelatin, which was quite delicious.

On arrival, the couple and I decided to rent rooms at the local Bali Hotel for one US dollar per night. There was no soap and no toilet paper, but the toilet worked. The French couple and I also decided to rent a car together (one dollar and fifty cents a day) and we took off to witness the preparations for a cremation ceremony that we had heard about. I learned that in Bali, the deceased is laid out and enclosed in a beautifully decorated palanquin, and carried around the village to ward off evil spirits, before the body and the palanquin are burned on a high platform, so everyone, in the village could witness it. Meanwhile, women were carrying huge bundles in a dishpan on their head containing three coconuts, a big bag of rice, and a decorated bowl on top, preparing for the ceremony.

I knew that Bali was now the only Hindu culture in Indonesia, influenced by Buddhism as well. Many Indian kingdoms had been in the archipelago in the past, but the country was mostly Muslim now, except for Bali. This made it unique. The Balinese were very artistic, as evidenced by their crafts and art, but also by the way they lived. Over the course of several days, I found myself buying a small old temple carving, a *kris* (dagger) with a beautifully carved handle and sheath, a bamboo copy of the Indian Ramayana in Balinese script, four small intricate bone carvings, and, of course, a handsome Balinese batik sarong. I later learned that Bali had no word for art.

We decided to go to a temple procession in Batuan nearby. While we waited for it to begin the French couple and I also indulged in some sweet round rice cakes, broken up and mixed with coconut pieces, then soaked in a jaggery syrup (a palm sap). Scrumptious. The drink that accompanied it I could only describe as tasting like tropical fragrances since I couldn't identify the flavors.

The most beautiful procession was awaiting us. A long line of women were walking with rice delicacies, fruit, cooked chicken and flowers beautifully arranged and balanced in high conical piles on their heads. Each was a little different, but all highly imaginative. From a distance they looked like a parade of many layered wedding cakes. It was breathtaking. The women were wearing colorful batik *kambens* (sarongs) and white lace *kebayas* (blouses), as they took offerings for the gods into the temple. We learned that we would be allowed to go into the temple if we wore a sarong over our clothes. We did, and inside an old woman was blessing both offerings and people with water from a jar mixed with flowers.

This event and the evening one we attended were certainly the highlight of my stay in Bali. That night the French couple and I watched the Legong dances. I could have been wrong, but I thought they appeared authentic, not just intended for tourists. Most everyone there, except us, looked to be Balinese. To my western eyes, the dances were absolutely tantalizing. Each female dancer had flowers worked into intricate gold headpieces. Two long scarves were wrapped around each young woman's breasts and waist, under which was a long sarong. The scarves had gold or silver threads running though the fabric so that they glistened in the evening lamplight. Their dances were elegant, angular, structured and slowly performed in bare feet, to a gamelan orchestra of brass xylophones.

I couldn't help but think: who was more civilized: the Balinese, or Americans? We had more technology but their culture was older, and focused on beauty, and less on time. Everyone knew their role and their place in the culture. Everything seemed to move smoothly. I later learned that traditional Balinese tried to avoid conflict to keep things in balance. I also learned that they valued the mountains, especially Mount Agung, the highest in Bali, because it was closest to the gods. Traditionally, the ocean was less sacred, unpredictable, and potentially dangerous. This certainly made it easier to attract tourism, since most tourists in the tropics were looking for beaches.

The next day we all moved out of our hotel to one on Kuta Beach—no electricity, but also no mosquitoes, it was lovely. The reason for the move: the night before a Balinese man at the Bali Hotel knocked on my door and demanded that I kiss him. I slammed the door in his face. Later, upon reflection, I realized that sexy American movies had probably given the Balinese the impression that all western women were easy. Still, I felt humiliated.

Another day passed and I checked in with the airlines, I was notified that the military were moving in and I needed to leave the following day. There were going to be military demonstrations at the airport. I didn't know why, but I took their word for it. Before heading to the airport, I walked along the beautiful huge breakers on the beach, picked up sand dollars, and said goodbye to the French couple. Then I waited at the airport for six hours and no plane arrived. I was furious because I was almost out of rupiahs. The exchange rate at the airport was unbelievably bad. The last straw was when an Indonesian man sneaked up on me in the airport's public ladies' bathroom, looking under the stall. Unnerved, I walked back to the hotel on Kuta Beach, checked into another room, and ate dinner with the French couple, who kindly exchanged my last rupiahs for dollars at a good rate. I do not know what I would have done without them.

The following morning the Electra jet was already at the airport, and I breathed a sigh of relief. We took off for Jakarta, and as we landed, we saw the first Malaysian Airways land there after three and a half years. Malaysian Prime Minister, Tun Razak, was there to sign the Bangkok agreement to end the Confrontation with Indonesia. A big procession from the embassies of both countries was present. The conflict came over the island of Borneo, part of which became the states of Sarawak and Sabah in the new country of Malaysia, created in 1963. The rest belonged to Indonesia.

Next stop, Bangkok, where my PCV friend, Wendy, and I met for the rest of our trip back to the US. At first we stayed in the lovely home of my godparents from Kansas, Marj and Jim, who worked for USAID. It was amazing to sleep in air-conditioned bedrooms, with clean filtered water on our bedside tables, with fresh cookies and red apples there at night. Marge showed us around Bangkok, along Sukhumvit Road, and to the old Oriental Hotel where many famous writers had stayed and written: Somerset Maugham, Joseph Conrad, James Michener and Paul Theroux, among others. We also stopped for lunch at the Erawan Hotel where we ate Thai food, sitting on the floor. And of course I shopped for Thai silk, mostly from the showhouses of Jim Thompson.

Buying cultural fabrics as we moved through Asia and Europe became my "thing." Fabrics or textiles were the least expensive artifacts I could buy, compared to silver or gold jewelry, carvings, or sculptures. They fit easily into my suitcase. They never broke. I could wear them when necessary, and they could be used as a cover for swimming in a river or taking a bath in public. Fabrics and heavier hand-woven textiles could serve as blankets or sheets when those weren't provided. Fabrics were indispensable to me while traveling.

Back in Bangkok, as I wrote earlier, Thompson had taken the traditional silk that the Thai were weaving and created a new silk for export. The colors were gorgeous. Thompson designed cottons as well, with traditional Thai motifs in beautiful colors. We visited his lovely Thai home, created from more than one Thai house, and full of antiques from Angkor to China. After he disappeared from the Cameron Highlands, in Malaysia, during the 1970s no one ever heard from him again, his fate unknown.

Soon, we'd had enough of busy Bangkok, so Wendy and I bought train tickets to head north to Chiang Mai. On the train we met three delightful French guys who were headed there to catch a boat down the Mekong River from Laos to Cambodia. Soon we all fell asleep in our individual compartments as the train chugged along to the highlands, and when we woke up in the morning we had arrived in Chiang Mai. We chose this northern city because it was known for its fine crafts, especially hammered silver. It was too expensive for me, but I enjoyed looking. We also considered heading up to meet members of the Hill Tribes on the border with China, but that turned out to be too expensive as well.

Instead we decided to take a country bus up to Chiang Dao to see the working elephants. We got off in pouring rain and when we arrived three elephants were stacking logs, so we sat in someone's jeep and took photos. It was fascinating as I had never seen elephants before. We then caught a lumber truck back to Chiang Mai, but, first sidetracked to a little village where we were invited into a simple Thai home of lovely people. I'm sure their life was hard, but this country seemed so gentle and peaceful compared to anywhere else I had been, with the exception of Bali.

The next day the weather in Chiang Mai was perfect. We rented bicycles and took off to visit temples inside a city moat within the old city walls. We also went to the US Air Force base to see if we could arrange to hitch a ride back to Bangkok when we were ready to go. No luck. Instead, by chance we met some missionaries, who said they would be happy to take us to meet the Karens, one of the Hill Tribes in Northern Thailand, with whom they were working. They took us to the base of a mountain where there was a Karen village. There we listened to worship services in Karen. Then, after I told them about the Mangyans whom I had worked with, we were all amazed to learn that both ethnic groups had similar creation stories—that human beings were originally born out of a man's leg. Obviously, something important had been carried over land and water from Northern Thailand, through Malaysia and Indonesia, on to the Philippines. It was wonderful to think about.

I noted that single girls wore white handwoven dresses and young men, red shirts. Married women wore black embroidered tops and red woven skirts. I bought one of each, since this was how they made money to buy things in town. That evening we went to a service where the Karen students sang and wore their traditional clothing.

The next day a couple of airmen we had earlier met at the base invited us to ride in their USAF truck for a trip up into the mountains to see Miao Hill Tribe members. Unfortunately, the truck got stuck in the mud so we had quite a walk up the mountain and back down. We thought we would never get out. But while there we were able to observe the Miao people. The Miao women wore short dresses or skirts, made from long blocks of material woven from the stem of a grass called *cogon* grass. The designs were waxed onto the cloth, which was dyed indigo blue. Then the women pleated the skirt, sewed it together and embroidered it. Everyone wore simple silver bands about their neck to protect them from evil spirits. They looked very Chinese in appearance to me and wore traditional Chinese frog closings on their jackets. But they also wore black hats with red topknots. They each seemed to have an opium pipe, a crossbow and a musical instrument of bamboo. This was a large village with houses that had thatched roofs and dirt floors. We were lucky to meet a woman who said she was a hundred and five.

On our final day in Chiang Mai, Wendy and I walked up to the top of a mountain to visit Doi Suthep Temple. We had a Thai guide who told us to bring candles and flowers as offerings. Unfortunately, once there, I used my foot to point to and inquire about a stone carving. The guide was horrified. I had crossed a line. He said you should never use your foot to point at anything. I apologized. The guide further informed me that one should never show the bottom of one's foot, which explained why women always sat sideways on the ground in their long sarongs with the soles of their feet facing away.

It was probably our earlier fraternizing with the airmen that finally got us a ride back to Bangkok. So, we packed up and went to the airport to wait for the air force plane to take off. It was a transport plane that we soon boarded, flying with the back end open. We sat on the side seats in the plane, buckled in most of the time, except for a brief visit to the cockpit. The two pilots asked us out once we landed. We did go out with them, but afterwards Wendy and I agreed that, at least for now, American guys bored us. We were ready to move on. So, the next day we packed everything up, shipped some stuff home, and made it to the airport in the nick of time. Next stop, Calcutta, India.

BANGKOK TO KATHMANDU VIA CALCUTTA

Wendy and I arrived in Calcutta on a hot and sultry night, and there were people sleeping on the streets, just as I was told there would be. Wendy and I found our way to a YWCA, where we felt comfortable, if guilty about those who had no bed, no home, no money. But Calcutta didn't depress me as much as I thought it might. I hated to see the poverty and deprivation, but at the same time I did not feel that anyone was envious of me, or were ready to jump me, or cheat me as a foreigner. We met nothing but cordiality in our contacts here and many went out of their way to help us.

One day, we took the train to Santiniketan, the home of the famous Indian poet, Tagore. Coming back to Calcutta in a yellow twilight, I saw India as full of stark and clashing colors, nothing subtle about it. The countryside looked as I had pictured it: flat with red dirt and some bright green patches, banyan trees, and mud huts with thatched roofs.

On that train ride, we met a lovely Armenian family. The Johannes befriended us and invited us to their home. There we were served pomelo (something like a big grapefruit), pear, cake, and tea. It was my first time to have tea with milk and it was surprisingly satisfying. Mr. Johannes owned a confectionary in the market. They took us to buy ice cream one evening where I saw a little boy on the street licking a discarded container. So I bought him an ice cream cone too. I was saddened, almost beyond belief, to witness a half-naked woman feeding her baby spoons full of water from the nearby gutter.

While in Calcutta, we visited Kalighat Temple, a Hindu Temple where people crowded around to make offerings and animal sacrifices to the goddess of destruction, Kali. We offered some rupees and were marked on the forehead with the red mark of the believer. We saw the tree of fertility where married women would bring a stone and hang it from a tree. When the woman had a child, she was to bring it back to the tree, after first washing herself in the river.

The night before we flew to Kathmandu, the Johanes family asked us over to say goodbye. We first went for a drive around the city with them, then listened to some records in their home, and ended the evening enjoying Indian sweets.

Five am saw us at the airport to catch the plane to Kathmandu. The windows were blacked out for military reasons, which surprised us. Also surprising was the bag lunch we were provided on board. We met a Nepalese young man on the plane, returning home after studying at the University of Hawaii, through the East West Center. Raj was charming and we promised to spend some time together. Meanwhile, upon arrival, Wendy and I made our way to the Peace Corps hostel. There, many American Volunteers were just hanging out. One of them was planning a fourteen-day trip through a pass in the Himalayas to a point twenty-five miles from the Tibetan border. It sounded tempting to us, but there was too much to consider before he left in a few days. While acknowledging that it would probably be the trip of a lifetime—something, to tell our grandchildren about—it would also be raining, muddy, cold and hot, with leeches, and mostly, exhausting. Instead we stayed in the Kathmandu valley which was very green and lush, grass even growing off the roofs of brick houses. It seemed a very quaint and colorful place.

The Nepalese men often appeared extremely handsome to me and the women were visually fascinating. The men wore interesting looking hats and a sort of jodhpur pants, while women wore a kind of saree that wrapped around them diagonally. The women often wore gold or silver nose rings and red streaks in their hair to indicate that they were married. There were many Tibetans in Kathmandu too, and the women wore black outfits like smocks, trimmed with red borders.

While we were in Nepal, the Peace Corps hostel closed for good, not just in Nepal, but across the world in countries with American Volunteers. I knew there was some concern that hostels attracted too many PCVs interacting together, when they were supposed to be spending more of their time with host country nationals. I kind of agreed with that, so, as we had no choice, we moved into the Snow View International Guest House.

One day Wendy and I rode bikes to the Tibetan refugee camp where we watched the weavers make their gorgeous and distinctive knotted and cut carpets. Those Tibetans lived in huts with prayer flags flying in the breeze overhead. While there we ran into two former Peace Corps Volunteers, John and Fred, who had worked in Ethiopia as lawyers. We spent the evening in town with them over supper, exchanging stories of our experiences in Africa and Southeast Asia. For dessert we practically inhaled some delicious cherry pie next door at The Pie Restaurant—American style. I couldn't imagine how the Nepalis came up with that idea…

The next morning we got up early to join Fred and John on a trip up to Nagarkot where it was possible to see Mount Everest at dawn before the mists rolled in. It was also where the summer palace of the king was. We first took a bus to Bhadgaon and walked across the plains for about an hour, then began climbing a mountain. We met interesting people along the way: a woman with newly born twins, and a baby glistening with oil, lying in the sun to toughen him up. We also sat in the rain on someone's porch and drank out of a brass jar. Men and women passed us with packs of wood on their backs. Finally, after a six-hour walk, we reached our bungalow in the pouring rain. As a result we stripped our soaking wet clothes and sat around in blankets from our rooms, enjoying hot tea and a big supper of rice and *dal*. At dusk the rain had stopped and we went outside to look at the opposite valley, which was just lovely.

The next morning we rose at five a.m. and opened our eyes to a string of snowcapped peaks, including Mount Everest. It was strikingly beautiful and well worth the trip. After a breakfast of crackers and hardboiled eggs, we trekked back to Bhadgaon in about four hours, sunburned, dirty and footsore, but each of us agreeing what a highpoint this trip was, literally and figuratively.

Raj, the Nepali we met on the plane, eventually contacted us and took us to Godavari to meet his family, his alma mater, and the botanical gardens. We had a delightful picnic with them which consisted of curried lamb, goats lungs, rooster's hearts, and some wine. It was actually good. That night in his village, Raj introduced us to dancing, comedy skits, and temple music which involved singing prayers with drums, bells, cymbals and a small organ. Soon, we said goodbye to Raj and his family, and later to John and Fred, as we prepared to resume our travels, back through India to Kabul, Afghanistan.

KATHMANDU TO KABUL VIA DELHI AND AGRA

On September 7, 1966, Wendy and I flew back to India, with a great view of the Himalayan mountain range from the air. It was almost seven weeks since our departure from the Philippines, as we landed in Benares. It seemed to us a crowded city, more like an overgrown town with cows, bicycles, rickshaws and oxcarts all over the streets. But everywhere the people seemed unaware of our passing by, except perhaps for an occasional child, who seemed to mock us. On the other hand, there were pleasant fragrances around us and no mosquitoes. The fried bread looked good and I was tempted.

We found an unclean room at the Palace Hotel for three rupees but we had to buy our own lock. And that was cheap, which helped to keep our trip to around one dollar US per day, and it was also right next to the Ganges River. Afterwards we spent the afternoon at the ruins of the Buddhist monastery where we saw the spot that Buddha had preached his first sermon, now a stupa with relics standing in his place in Sarnath.

I learned that in India Hinduism had existed since about 2,000 B.C. and Buddhism was born in the sixth century B.C. I also learned that most Indians were not Buddhist, but Hindu, because, according to our guide, "Buddhists didn't like to worship and also because Buddhism frowned on too many children." I wasn't sure about his answer, but at the time I knew nothing else. Buddhism, meanwhile, fled to flourish in the Asian countries of Sri Lanka, Burma, and Thailand.

The next morning we got up early and walked to the Ganges River. Along the way, beggars were all lined up. Down at the *Ghats* (steps) beside the river people were bathing, drinking, praying, and brushing their teeth. We decided to hire a guide with a boat so that we could ride down the river and get an overview of all the activities on it. We saw four or five cremations happening on the ghats, with visible burned skin and bones, all of which gave off a foul odor. I understood to visit the Ganges, bathe in it and be cremated there was the wish of most Hindus. It was a sacred river.

Meanwhile, we tried to visit several temples, but the men inside were hostile and threw us out. Somehow we had crossed a line of significance that we didn't understand. Instead we walked along the backstreets to the local bazaar. There we saw people selling what looked like red and orange dust, lots of Indian foods and flowers for offerings. I found a brass plate, cup and spoon, fork and knife that I bought because I liked their elegant simplicity. Soon we were hungry and ended up at the Benares Clark's Hotel, where we had high tea. There we met a family traveling from Malaysia with two small daughters. They encouraged us to join them and we had a delightful time. They were happy to learn that I had spent time in their country.

After a few days, we set off for Agra, to see the Taj Mahal. Arriving in the evening, we were still able to get someone to take us to see the memorial. No moon, hardly any stars, mostly just clouds, so that it appeared to be a phantom. The guide took us through by lantern light, a very eerie experience. There were eighty foot ceilings which helped cause as many as fifteen echoes, as we talked softly and walked through. He said that the Taj Mahal was built between 1631 and 1649 in white marble, by the Shah Jahan for his favorite wife, following her death. Flower shapes were created with semi-precious stones of jade, agate, and jasper embedded in the marble throughout. The cost of the Taj Mahal was estimated at forty million US dollars. The building had a view over the Yamuna river, to the proposed black marble tomb intended for the Shah Jahan himself, with just the foundation laid. It was never finished.

After finding a place to sleep at the inexpensive Agra Hotel, we woke early the next morning and returned to the Taj. Although there was no pink sunrise, it looked stunning in the light. Next we visited the tomb that the Shah Jahan's wife built. There her parents, her grandparents, and sisters were placed. It was smaller and less overwhelming, but more complicated in detail than the Taj, later becoming the Taj Mahal's model.

Before heading on to New Delhi, a guide showed us the Agra Fort, built in the time of Akbar, the grandfather of Shah Jahan, to protect them from the Moguls. Akbar was of Chinese descent, and within the Fort walls he built small marble palaces for every member of his family, all done in marble and inlaid with the same semi-precious stones as the Taj. Containing convex mirrors, the Shah Jahan's palace included a bath with both hot and cold water. A waterfall flowed into a perfumed fountain. There was also a tunnel from the Shah's palace to the Taj Mahal. Because the Shah was semi-blind later in life, a mirror was placed in the palace that reflected the Taj. In the end, the Shah's son held him for seven years until his death, and had his body carried through the underground tunnel to the Taj Mahal for burial next to his wife. I found all of this both touching and amazing—so much wealth, so much display. But the truth was that I was a captive audience.

Amidst all of this beauty and extravagance, I noted there seemed to be a lot of anti-American sentiment in India. No doubt some of that negativity was due to our intervention in Vietnam. There were even anti-Peace Corps feelings that some Indians had frankly spoken to us about. I can't remember the details, but it hit us hard, probably because in 1966 we still felt idealistic about our country, and certainly the Peace Corps. As a relatively naïve young person,

I always believed that our government took the high moral route on most everything.

New Delhi appeared modern and sophisticated. Yet I knew that poor people lived just behind the biggest buildings in the downtown. Meanwhile, we kept running into other Volunteers, including one young woman who worked in poultry in India, and a young man named Raj, working for the U.N. in Egypt. We seemed to attract a lot of young men. We encountered a Sikh man named Surander, who invited Wendy and me to join a couple of other guys for dinner. One was his friend, another Sikh in the Indian Air Force named Kajer, the other a Chinese engineering student. They seemed kind of young, and tended to act a little fresh with us, which I disliked. At any rate, we did have a delicious Indian dinner of chicken *tandoori*, accompanied by naan, curries, dal, a curd with sesame seeds, and something with anise for dessert. I loved Indian food.

Despite my misgivings, the next day Kajer and Surander invited us to spend the day going around New Delhi on their motor bikes. We actually had a great time. I had never been on a motor bike before, though onlookers must have thought it a funny sight: an American girl sitting behind a Sikh with Air Force goggles on.

Afterwards, we visited a temple before eating paratha bread and *chana* (curried beans) in Old Delhi. Wendy and I ended up having an argument with the Hindu guide at a temple. We wanted to know if there were so many starving people in India, why didn't they kill the cows for food? Since I understood that there were twice as many cows as people, it would supposedly feed the population for years. I don't know where I got that statistic, but I must have heard it to use it so flagrantly with the guide. His response was that cows were considered more sacred than people. Besides, he said, not a single person was dying of hunger, which I found almost too much to believe. I said that hunger happened in every country, including the US. But, I couldn't convince him, and maybe shouldn't have, considering he may have been reflecting the beliefs of many Hindus.

I asked Kajer what it meant to be a Sikh. He said Sikhs were the original warrior class of India. They never cut their hair so that they wouldn't need extra people to help them during war. The result was that they covered their hair with a turban instead. Little boys even wore ribbons in their hair. They also wore a steel (formerly iron) bracelet which could be used in war to break a nose. They weren't supposed to dance, smoke, or sing, either, but they often did. While I was talking, Kajer asked if he could tell my fortune, so I gave him my hand. He said I would have a long life, difficult at the end, no affairs, one love, one marriage, and I would be stable and happy, with good support for my life and at least three children.

That evening we had our last Indian dinner together with Surander and Kajer at the Kwality Restaurant in Old Delhi. Later I sat outside on the balcony at the YMCA Tourist Hostel, cooling off with the distinct fragrance of jasmine in the air. Looking down at the street, I could see a few sarees of muted hues passing by in the evening. It was our last night in India and I had mixed feelings about the country, that I wasn't able to process completely yet. The next day we were leaving for Kabul, Afghanistan.

India looked hot and flat as we flew over India and Lahore, Pakistan, but Afghanistan was another story. Our first view of the Hindu Kush was like seeing the Grand Canyon lying on its side. The color looked like a black and white movie that had turned grey. It had a fantastic blandness to it, but, though dull, was fascinating to me. It was actually blinding to look at from the air. I could imagine the scorching heat below, but was soon surprised: It was only seventy-five degrees. Delightful, clean, and wide open was our first impression of Kabul. The men looked in good health and had an air of confidence about them. Of course we hadn't seen very tall men in a long time. The Afghan men were wearing beige cotton wrapped turbans on their heads with trailing ends. They were wearing vests trimmed in gold braid, richly woven, striped shepherd coats off the shoulder, with long shirts and baggy pants. The many women we saw on the streets were wearing *chadri*, a robe over their head with mesh material in front of their eyes.

We headed to the Press Club hotel at US$1.25 per night. We

happened to walk right in on an Afghani wedding in the hotel and were invited to join in. The bride was wearing a short green dress with a veil covering her face and the groom was looking very sober sitting beside her. Girls of all ages presented themselves to the couple and danced with hesitation steps and seductive movements of their shoulders and hands. Then everyone went into a large banquet hall and literally filled their faces at platters along a long line of tables. I especially enjoyed the unleavened bread, sweet grapes, fresh peaches and honeydew melon. We had not seen fruits like that in a long time.

The next night we were invited to dinner at the Khyber Restaurant where we seriously indulged. It was the most American place I had seen in our travels through Asia. Big lusty salads, pies, cakes, and meat dishes, all served cafeteria style. It was almost unbelievable. And the strawberries were the most luscious I could remember. Unfortunately, we also got rushed by some Afghani men, but our host, Logan, a former PCV in Afghanistan, staved them off.

The next morning we couldn't resist breakfast at the Khyber Restaurant again. We had some Persian pecan rolls which were to die for. Later Logan took us to lunch among the Russians at the Springer Hotel. The Russians looked just as I thought they would. But I was most interested in the lunch of cold strawberry soup and strawberry pie. Afterwards we took in a movie, noting that the audience was all men. It was a strange feeling to be surrounded by handsome, yet slightly ominous looking men, at least to me. We knew we were being a little provocative, without the cover of a woman's chadri, compared to Afghani women, so we were grateful for Logan's presence.

The rest of the day I was not feeling so well, so I went back to my room and spent the day in bed with a fever. The following day I went to see the Peace Corps doctor in Kabul. For the next four days I lay flat on my back in bed with diarrhea, headaches and hurting eyes. I only got up to go to the bathroom or vomit out the window, because the only bathroom was a long way down the hall. I couldn't eat a thing. The doctor gave me lots of pills and a couple of shots but I didn't feel better until we were about to fly to Tehran. I am pretty sure it was the strawberries, if not the lettuce, perhaps fertilized in human excrement.

Meanwhile, Wendy went out with her newly acquired Afghani friends in my absence. She was a little vulnerable on her own, and had several proposals of marriage. Both of us felt terrible that we hadn't seen any of Afghanistan, not even much of its capitol. We were especially sorry not to visit Bamian to see the giant Buddhas carved out of a cliff.

I had made an earlier prediction that we might have to skip the Middle East and go straight to Europe. Then I was thinking of money, but this time I was thinking of health as well. We did spend a night in Tehran, Iran, only because Pan Am couldn't get us to Athens in one day. So they put us up at the Tehran Palace Hotel with free food and lodging for one night. We spent the afternoon walking around the city and found it modern, but somewhat nondescript, rather unexciting. With little time, we obviously saw only a small part of the city. We regretted, since we were here, not visiting Isfahan or Persepolis. But, it was impossible to do everything we had hoped for. I had one hundred and eighty US dollars-worth of Travelers Checks left in my purse, and all of Europe to go. It was September 22, 1966, and I had traveled for sixty-five days.

KABUL TO ATHENS

It was four-thirty a.m. We flew over the Fertile Crescent, the Tigris Euphrates Valley, then dipped and turned over the Mediterranean and flew back into the morning. Beirut was shining in the sun-tipped cloudburst of dawn, a sight to behold—we were headed toward the European frontier at last.

Flying to Athens, we were excited to see how the western half of the world lived and looking forward to the few short weeks that we had left before hitting the United States. We were full of enthusiasm. The stopover in the Beirut airport looked beautiful, but so did Athens. I got my first view of the Acropolis from the air, a great surging feeling. Wendy and I went through culture shock seeing all of the modern stores and beautiful tall women. The life was fast paced for us, but everyone said it was slower here than anywhere in Europe. After we went for our mail at American Express, letters from my Filipino family had me sitting down for a homesick cry over all those people I had left behind.

Once I recovered, we checked into a YWCA and dumped our bags. We went outside to look around and stopped at a sidewalk café. Two Greek guys named Andres and Peter started talking to us and invited us out for the evening. It seemed safe enough and we accepted. That evening we climbed to the highest point in Athens, up a small mountain called Philopappus. We walked and joked and laughed at their English, all in good fun. Then they took us to Old Athens at the foot of the Acropolis to an open air night club. We drank Greek wine, and ate bread and melon.

The next day we slept until noon because we'd been up for twenty-four hours the day before. We had delicious Greek cheese pie for lunch—the food and water were superb. I couldn't wait to see the Agora and the Acropolis, to see how they compared to my college art books. They were just as wonderful as I had imagined, a great feeling to see these places in person. At the Archeological Museum, we saw original statues of Poseidon, the Jockey, Hermes, and Paris. I loved it. Afterwards we stopped at a little Greek sidewalk café and had shish kebobs, coleslaw in yogurt, fresh bread and coffee, then got hit for two dollars US. It seemed like a fortune to us at the time.

Meanwhile, our evenings continued to be full. American girls seemed to be in great demand in Athens, much to our surprise. Maybe they thought we would be easy, and if so, they must have been disappointed. We met Andres and Peter again on the street, and they took us out to a Whisky A Go Go place where we had a wonderful time dancing and sipping vermouth. I had rested that afternoon and was in a state of happy abandon all evening, enjoying everything to the utmost.

At American Express the next day I met a young man named Constantino, who said one of his parents was Greek and the other

Italian. Most people called him Dino. We sat at the nearby café and talked for a long time. I found him very interesting, but because we were meeting Andres and Peter I turned down his invitation for dinner. With Peter and Andres we walked around old Athens again, drank something that tasted like licorice and ate salami, goat cheese, and fresh olives. Greeks ate everywhere in open air cafes. We especially loved the cheese and chicken pies, grapes, tomatoes and ouzo wine. Our favorite place to be was Constitution Square where it was great fun to watch everyone in Athens walk by.

Wendy and I decided to take a student classical tour, five days for US twenty-two dollars. On the first day, outside the bus, I ran into my German friend, Renate. I had no idea she was in Greece and that we would be on the same tour. A happy accident. Now I didn't need to travel to Germany as I had planned. So, we all took off together and visited the Monastery at Daphni. We saw beautiful mosaics set in a gold background, all the things I'd seen in the art books, eleventh century artifacts, beautiful draperies with beautiful bodies underneath, from the Byzantine Period. We then drove through Thebes, the setting for the legend of Oedipus Rex. Greece had so many historic sites, I chose only a few stories connected to ancient Greece to relate here, all based on our guide's description.

The first story occurred in Delphi, the name translating into the dolphin. The Apollo temple sat five hundred meters above sea level on the slopes of Mount Parnassus, the home of Apollo. We saw the remains of the Athenian treasury as we walked the Sacred Way. It was mind blowing. I especially loved the statue called the Charioteer of Delphi, a beautiful green bronze with lovely feet and the eyes still intact. A symbolic sculpture called "the navel of the world" depicted mother earth in Delphi as the place where the Greeks drew their strength.

The story has it that in ancient times, the priestess at the Apollo Temple, originally called Sybil, was a young girl who had to purify herself in the springs. Later, she was abducted, causing a scandal, so thenceforth an older woman was always selected and dressed as a young girl. As a result of fumes shooting up from the earth, the priestess easily went into a trance. She answered any individual's questions from the city state, but always in riddles with double meanings so that the oracle was never wrong.

The next day the guide told us the story of Cranus, the old god and his wife, Rhea. The oracle said one of his children would kill him, so Cranus swallowed them all, one by one. But Rhea saved her son Zeus and left him on the isle of Crete. In his stead she gave Cranus a stone wrapped in swaddling clothes to swallow. Later, Zeus came back, overthrew his father and made him regurgitate all his brothers and sisters, including the stone, which became the navel at Delphi. The Temple of Zeus enclosed, at one time, a fifteen meter statue of Zeus, created with ivory and gold, and studded with diamond eyes. It was later stolen by the Turks and landed in Istanbul. Eventually an earthquake toppled the columns of the Temple.

Finally, we visited the Athena temple where the Greek athletes trained for the Olympics. We learned that the Olympics were started in the eighth century BC, and ended in the third century AD, because the Greeks were pagan, and Christianity had started to take hold. In the 1800s a Frenchman revived the Olympics, and held them in Athens. The Olympiads became the years between the games. On the day we visited the stadium in Olympia—still the original—we learned that it had held 70,000 people, all men, seated on the earth terraces. One story said that the only known woman to ever see her son win the Olympics, was a woman called Caliphates, from Rhodes, who disguised herself as a man.

Outside the stadium, inscriptions in stone represented those who had bribed or cheated when they were caught. Winning the games three times allowed a man to erect a statue of himself, and he was henceforth considered immortal. Later, the Romans under Emperor Nero joined in the games as brothers of the free Greeks. Nero even won once. He also added music and poetry to the competition, the only prize, a wreath fashioned from an olive branch. The flame, created with a glass lens and the sun, always led the way to the Olympics.

We saw so many sites on this tour, I couldn't begin to mention them all. Highlights included Atlas and Athena together holding up the heavens; the ancient lion gate built at Mycenae; the pedestal where the Apostle Paul preached on the bema in the agora of Corinth; the fate of Persephone, daughter of the goddess of agriculture, who ate a pomegranate and was banned, only later to be allowed back six months of every year during which crops bloomed, and in the other six months her mother mourned and nothing grew. Thus, the seasons were explained.

The participants on the tour were extremely diverse. I loved the mixture of people: a beautiful Swiss woman and her German husband, an American Chinese, a Peace Corps couple from Turkey, a Massachusetts woman married to a Greek who came back to meet his family, a Thai woman, an Indian painter, and a Hawaiian woman living in Switzerland, among others, including my friend Renate. We spent a lot of time together interacting during lunch and dinners at our hotels en route. We shared fresh bread from the countryside, cheeses we bought, and peaches at each stop. It was an interesting time for me. I was beginning to ease back into life in the West. And Greece was the perfect place to do that, with its position as the birth of democracy and western culture.

Upon our return to Athens, Peter and Andres were there to meet us and take us to dinner. I turned down the invitation this time because I wanted to spend some time talking to Dino. I waited again at the café in front of the American Express office and eventually Dino showed up. That night we went to a very plush nightclub and had a wonderful time talking and connecting as if we were old friends, followed by a spaghetti dinner just before midnight. Afterwards, I hurried back to the Y because I had learned the matron who guarded the entrance chastised young women who got in late, for their presumed lack of moral integrity.

After a short night of sleep, early the next morning Wendy and I packed our bags and Dino saw us off at the airport. I was sorry to leave Athens, but our budget restraints forced us to move on, so we were off to Rome.

ATHENS TO ROME AND FLORENCE

Italy looked lovely from the air, but Rome looked expensive. Upon arrival, we got a room in a place called Liliana Pensione. We dropped our bags off, started to change our clothes, and then discovered we had accidentally locked ourselves in our room. We couldn't unlock the door so we rang the bell, shouted for help, and knocked loudly on the door. Finally, an Italian gentleman came by and we pushed the key under the door for him. Fortunately he got it open. But he must have been surprised to see two girls barely dressed, standing there. Perhaps he thought it was the newest approach to lure a man into a woman's room. But the next thing we heard was that the couple down the hall were also locked in.

In Rome we could eat for about one hundred lira (twenty-eight US cents) for a fixed price meal of minestrone soup, bread, wine, tomato salad, fruit or cheese, and chicken or beef steak. We walked around that first day enjoying the beautiful fountains, arches, Renaissance buildings, Baroque churches and sculpture. It led us to the Vatican, which was just as I had pictured it. I loved the enormous statement the baroque Bernini canopy made above the altar, and finally, just before exiting the Cathedral, Michelangelo's *Pieta*, which was much smaller than I imagined, but just as lovely. But most of all, I was impressed with the magnificence of the figures by Michelangelo on the ceiling of the Sistine Chapel.

As we continued our walk around Rome, we stopped to eat pizza for lunch, then went to the Pantheon, the oldest preserved building in Rome, a beautifully harmonious piece of architecture built in 27 B.C. The bronze roof was apparently melted down for St. Peter's canopy. Amazing.

As in Greece, there were too many sites to mention as we walked the streets of Rome. No one tried to pick us up as in Athens, though our bottoms were pinched a few times, which I understood as typical behavior of young Roman men. A bit uncomfortable to experience, but we were supposed to take it as a compliment. Most men were gentlemen and helped us when we got lost. Meanwhile, we visited the Diocletian Baths which housed 3,000 in ancient

When in Rome we visited many of the noted ancient sites including the Colosseum still the largest amphitheater ever built and despite its age still the largest standing today.

times; sixteen ancient Egyptian columns; the Palatine Hill where aqueducts originated; the Roman Forum; the place where Julius Cesar was cremated and his rostrum; and, of course, the Colosseum. It was exciting to think that Caesar and Cleopatra must once have walked there.

Sightseeing was tiring so I took some time off and got my haircut, and we stopped for lasagna for dinner. The rest of the day, we went shopping and I treated myself by buying a very sophisticated looking pink wool dress. Wendy bought a cashmere sweater, fancy underwear and some new fashion shoes with thick heels, which I thought were horrid. Before departing Rome we went to St. Peter's Cathedral for Mass. The organ music was beyond impressive. Afterwards we stood out in the piazza and watched Pope Paul bless the crowd from the window of his mansion. Later we each threw three coins in the Fountain of Trevi, pretty much a requirement while in Rome. We got caught in the rain and finally ducked into an eating place where we met two Guatemalans. It was fun trying to communicate. We ended the evening and our time in Rome by having coffee on the Via Veneto, and singing "Arrivederci Roma" in two part harmony, all the way back to our pensione.

The train ride to Florence was easy. That night, from the end of the street at our new *pensione*, I could see the cathedral called the Duomo. I was so impressed. It was more beautiful than words could describe, or pictures could show. Afterward we went to The Red Garter for a jazz jam session. I realized I hadn't seen any beautiful Italian women yet. Somehow I expected them to be very beautiful, but I hadn't encountered any who fit that description. How could that be?

The next morning, I walked to the Cathedral and climbed to the dome. In the Uffizi gallery I was able to see the famous painting, *Venus* by Botticelli, and many other treasures. Later we walked to the Medici Chapel where Michelangelo's *Dawn and Dusk, Night and Day* statues were on display. We visited the Laurentian Library which had original letters and manuscripts by Dante, Petrarch, Napoleon and other famous figures. There we met the editor of the *National Book Review* who bought us each a slide of an original letter, and took us to lunch.

Our final day was another good day as we walked across the Ponte Vecchio, a bridge built in Etruscan times. We ended up viewing the unfinished statues of Michelangelo and the tender, but strong, statue of *David*. It nearly brought me to tears. I had seen the statue in art history books, but in person it was stunning, breathtaking. Later we visited Michelangelo's house with his early works and his drawings on exhibit. Finally we walked to the Santa Croce Church where Dante and Michelangelo were both buried. So much talent in one place.

We made a side trip to Pisa before flying to Paris, spending the day near Pisa's Leaning Tower. It seemed a quaint Romanesque place and I was enchanted. Our flight to Paris took us through Milan. For the first time I was worried as to whether we'd make it through rough weather, or not. The Milan Airport was huge, but the Orly airport in Paris was larger. Between the two, I lost my bag of presents and the white suede Afghan coat I bought in Kabul. It was not cured and smelled like rotting meat, anyway. No doubt it had probably been taken off the plane and thrown away somewhere.

FLORENCE TO NEW YORK VIA PARIS

Paris sparkled from the air by night. We found a hotel for three US dollars, which was too much, but what could we do? It was on the Rue de Seine on the Left Bank, so a better place for seeing the sights would be hard to find. In the morning we walked across the Seine river to the Louvre museum where we spent the whole day. They had a great collection of Egyptian and Mesopotamian art, and Greek pottery. Most of the statues were copies except the *Winged Victory* and the *Venus de Milo*. I was disappointed in the *Mona Lisa*. It was so small, I wondered why it was so famous. That evening we walked to the Notre Dame Cathedral and heard a mass in its lovely interior.

I had fun trying to speak French but was beginning to feel restless, lonely and eager to get home. That night we walked up to the Sacre Coeur with a great view over Paris. There we were attacked verbally by young Parisians who recognized us as Americans. They criticized us for being involved in the Vietnam War. I was speechless and hurt. I knew very little about the Vietnam War and had nothing to do with its origins. I had just been a Peace Corps Volunteer for two years in the Philippines. Wendy and I both ended up crying, so we left and walked back down to our hotel.

The next day, we talked about what had happened, our general need to get home, and our lack of money. We felt it was time to make arrangements to return to the US the next day. At the airport we made the reservations, only to find out we each owed five US dollars for airport fees. That meant we couldn't pay our last night in the hotel. The Boston couple behind us heard everything. They pulled out a twenty dollar bill and gave it to us. We were most grateful and asked for their address so that we could write them a thank you note. They refused and told us, just to take it and enjoy your last day. We were flabbergasted and celebrated by attending the Paris Opera that night. I went in my new dress from Rome, with gloves from Florence, and my sweater from Hong Kong. *La Traviata* was beautiful, my first time to see an opera.

On our way back to our hotel that night we met some college kids selling newspapers. We told them we were too poor, so they gave us one. We stopped for a coffee at an outside café and met an artist who was poorer than us. So we gave him a little money for a small painting on paper. Thus ended our time in Europe.

The next day, we boarded a giant Pan Am plane that took us to La Guardia Airport in New York City. When we landed and entered customs, we could see Wendy's parents calling down to us from the balcony above. It was easy to pass customs and Wendy's parents greeted both of us with hugs. They took us for lunch at the airport café where I had a hamburger with blueberry pie a la mode. It was a duplicate of my last meal in Honolulu before flying off to the Philippines. I still had another couple of months and the whole American continent to go, visiting with friends and family. My parents had sent a little more money, so I was soon on my way back to Honolulu, full circle. It was October 19, 1966.

Malaysia

The author with Nate, six-month-old Windi, and our dog Thumper, outside our second home in Malaysia. This is the outfit I had made for the Sultan's birthday party.

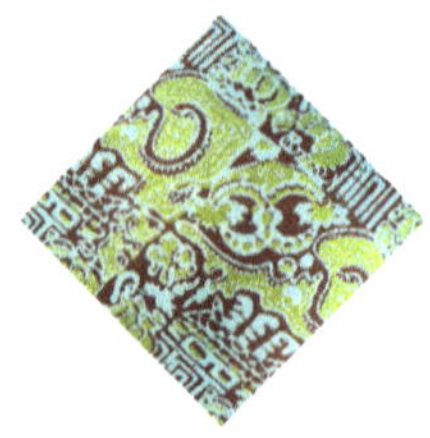

KUANTAN, PAHANG, MALAYSIA

Twenty-six-years-old and married for six months, I landed with my husband, Nate, at Subang International Airport outside the capital of Kuala Lumpur in June of 1969. Having visited here once as a Peace Corps Volunteer, I had admired the batik paintings, and eaten my first curry. But now Nate and I were going to live here for two or more years. I was thrilled.

We were sent almost immediately to our post in Kuantan, where Nate would be the Peace Corps Representative along the coast of East Malaya. He was in charge of about ninety volunteers living and working there. I, on the other hand, was not allowed to work. It was illegal. The concern was that I might take a job from a Malaysian citizen. Instead, I was called a "non-matrix spouse" by the US government. I didn't really care because I could accompany Nate everywhere he traveled on behalf of the Volunteers.

First, we had to settle into our house. We were assigned to a concrete box in a *cul de sac* of similar structures on *Jalan Datu Mahmud*. It was big enough to have four bedrooms, two bathrooms, a living/dining room, and a kitchen. The double front doors could open to the outside and would be protected with a folding iron gate. Peace Corps provided the house and all of the furnishings—simple beds, a fan, a table with chairs, plus comfortable bamboo chairs and a sofa in the living room. Our bedroom was on the hotter east side of the house, and on a weekend when we wanted to sleep in, we would just switch mid-morning to the bedroom on the west side where it was cooler. I was happy, even though the landlord had forbidden us to eat the ripe mangoes on the tree in the garden.

Our first disappointment came when we were informed that

all of our shipment of clothing and personal items had been hijacked on the road between KL and Kuantan. The hijacker had stopped a lorry in the middle of the night and tied the driver to a rubber tree, then taken off with the lorry and all its goods. Our biggest losses were the sum total of the personal slides and photos we had each taken as former PCVs, Nate in Thailand and me in the Philippines, including my long trip home through Asia and Europe. We had not shared them with each other yet, so it was a devastating blow. We never saw the contents of our shipment again, except—ironically—one slide from the official investigation. That's how we knew it was our shipment. We never got over this loss.

Life in Kuantan was interesting and fun. We soon had our favorite places to eat. We often had *kway teow,* a wide noodle soup, for lunch in the shop opposite Nate's office. For dinner sometimes we went downtown to an Indian restaurant that served *nasi biriyani*, a complete dinner on banana leaves. Then there was always the open air market where you could eat great Chinese stir-fried meals, or a Malay curry, like *kari ikan* or *kari ayam*, or even beef *rendang*. When we ate at home, I had to rely heavily on Cold Storage and Hock Lee's for imported items, since I didn't have much experience in cooking, either American, or much less, Malaysian style. But I could make grilled cheese sandwiches with cheap American cheese, which I did on Saturdays for our lunch. This was always accompanied by a couple of small bottles of coke poured over a glass from the freezer, which had previously been half-filled with water, and turned into ice.

Meanwhile, we soon took off on our first trips to visit Volunteers. Nate had the use of an old grey Land Rover with metal benches in the back. It was great. During many trips north, we stopped at beautiful beaches, including one special empty one called Gebeng, to which we returned often. It faced a long current that came down from Japan, skirting Vietnam along the way. We knew this because, not only were there old casts and medical detritus from the ongoing Vietnam War, but also beautiful glass balls used to float fishing nets in Japan. Very few were broken, but over time we collected only the best ones and kept them in a big market basket.

We also visited wonderful small rural shops with intricate woven sleeping mats near Kuala Terengganu, and beautiful silver filigree jewelry and delicate paper kites in Kota Bharu. And everywhere you could find lovely Malaysian batik cloth which I bought to replace all the clothes I had lost. And, of course the food at each stop was wonderfully delicious. Kuala Terengganu was known for its *ikan merah*, but I loved the Indian *roti chenai* with a curry even more. Sometimes we were lucky to find shark's fin soup with vinegar—beyond delicious. Occasionally you would even get *gula melaka* for dessert too. The only notable exceptions were the breakfasts at the old British Rest Houses, where we often stayed. The rooms were simple, with mosquito nets and a fan, if you were lucky. Always in a stunning location with a view of the mountains or the ocean, these quiet rest houses were a retreat for us. But the breakfasts were dark dry toast, marmalade, cold eggs, and sweetened condensed milk flavored with coffee. Still, it was all part of the experience of living in Malaysia.

The PCVs usually lived in wooden houses on raised stilts, often shaded by palms and cooled by sea breezes, just like their Malay counterparts. The Volunteers almost never had running water, indoor bathrooms or electricity. They worked in fisheries and taught school, got around on bikes, tri-shaws, or simply walked. Ironically, when they had to go to KL on business or vacation, they were driven by Mercedes Benz taxis. These were the only kind of taxis available and we all took them when necessary. They took off only when they were full, meaning at least four people in the back seat, and two, plus the driver, in the front. In that scenario, people mixed with big bundles and babies, made the ride not as luxurious as it sounded.

Most of the Volunteer's counterparts did have motorcycles, which the PCVs were not allowed. I assumed that had to do with safety for Volunteers, decided back in Washington, DC, perhaps. However, this became a huge issue with some Volunteers. Many purchased motorcycles surreptitiously. When Nate found out, he was supposed to take them. As a result we occasionally had more than one in our dining room, hidden behind a batik screen.

The author with Nate and Windi, plus our good Malaysian friends, Sarasa and Bala, visiting our camp on Kennebago Lake, Maine, 1973.

We soon began to make friends of our own. Nate met Bala because he worked in fisheries, and when I met his wife, Sarasa, we became great friends. When I had a fungus on my foot, they directed me to Dr. Mahalingam, and eventually we met his wife too and enjoyed many social occasions. There was another Indian woman doctor in our neighborhood who dined every evening with her fiancé. Sometimes we joined them, but both their parents forbid a marriage because he was Hindu and she was Muslim. Our Malay neighbors across the street were lovely, Zakinah and Noordin. They were well educated and energetic.

Another neighbor befriended me, a delightful Chinese Malaysian named Kim. She introduced me to mahjong. I also joined an exercise class in her home every week. She was lovely, but her husband was a less than friendly Australian. Once, in a drunken state, he told Nate

Nate, pulling out of our driveway in our 1948 MG TC, in Kuantan, Pahang, Malaysia. We bought it for $500 US in 1969.

that he should be a member of the local expatriate Kuantan Club—a holdout from the days of British colonialism—and even be president by now. We were not really interested, plus joining such clubs was frowned upon by the Peace Corps.

Meanwhile, since I wasn't allowed to drive the Peace Corps Land Rover, I looked for another car. Incredibly, I found a jungle green 1948 British MG TC for sale at five hundred US dollars. What a great deal I thought, so naturally I bought it. I really loved that little car, easy to drive and run errands around Kuantan. Of course, Malaysians drove on the left side of the road which took a while—and several near tragic right turns—to get used to.

By 1971, I was pregnant and looked for a doctor in Kuantan to deliver our baby. The doctor at the local hospital I met was afraid of possible repercussions in treating a foreign woman, I suspected. He urged me to go to Kuala Lumpur and get an obstetrician there. So, at the hospital in Petaling Jaya near KL, I found a doctor who was half Chinese and half British. He was perfect, I thought. When the time came, I was ushered into a large circular room, with curtained areas fanning off from the center. Behind those curtains were women at different stages of delivering babies. Everyone was very quiet. In the center was the emergency equipment available for all the doctors to share, if needed. I thought it seemed like a pretty logical system. Luckily, I had a fairly normal delivery, and Nate was able to photograph the whole experience. Our daughter, Windi Tai-Alae Bowditch, was born at 12:20 pm on April 1, 1971. To the shock of several of our friends and relatives, we used a photo of her being born on the birth announcement. We also quoted words from a song by The Moody Blues called "Have You Heard?"

Windi's name became a big question for everyone. It was clearly outside of naming traditions in the U.S. But that was part of the point, as we felt free to name her as we pleased, living in another country. It actually all started at a mahjong game with friends in Kuantan. In mahjong there's a run called The Windy Chow. Our friends joked that we should name our daughter Windy Chow Bowditch. I laughed, but Nate thought Windy was a great name for a girl. I was sure we were expecting a boy, based on how my Malaysian friends said I was carrying the baby. So we had a boy's name honoring a Malay friend named Mokhtar, but we hadn't chosen a girl's name. So, I agreed, that if the baby was a girl we could name her Windi, spelling it with an "i" at the end. When thinking about a middle name, two possibilities came to me. I liked Tai, which meant free in Thailand, where Nate served as a Volunteer. The other was Alae, which I remembered as the name of a tiny island off the coast of Maui. It had been the place where Nate said he thought he would like to marry me. How perfect that Alae meant "the place that parts the wind." The combination of names seemed to go together perfectly. Years later I learned that the island's name was actually Alau, which meant mud hen in Hawaiian, but I continued to believe in Alae as "the place that parts the wind."

THE PAHANG RIVER & THE SULTAN'S BIRTHDAY PARTY

The Pahang River bordered the state of Pahang and entered the ocean in a blur of water, sand and mud. One day Nate and I decided to swim down the end of the river to the ocean's shore. We were each carrying something over our head while swimming on our backs, as we navigated the current. I remember I was carrying our new Panasonic radio bought in Hong Kong. We made it, but it was a crazy thing to do. Near the end I just wanted to jettison the heavy radio into the water.

We loved living in Kuantan near the ocean and often came to the beach to swim. In 1969 most Malaysians preferred not to go in the water and stared at us instead. I did occasionally see snakes swimming in it, which should have warned me. Nate liked to fish off the rocks at the end of the beach while I sunbathed. The first time we brought our six-month-old daughter here, she immediately took a clump of sand and put it in her mouth.

Kuantan was also the home of the Sultan of Pahang, the hereditary constitutional head of the state. The Sultan and the majority of Malays were Muslim and could not believe that our astronauts had only recently landed on the moon. We also heard that Muslim men were allowed three wives on the land, any more would have to live on the water. Although we didn't hang out with the Sultan, Nate's position as the U.S. Peace Corps Representative for the East Coast of the Malay peninsula in Kuantan, put him on the official map.

Our second year there Nate got an formal invitation to the Sultan's birthday party. It read to Mr. Nathaniel Bowditch, *dan isteri.* That meant he could bring his wife. I was thrilled to go to such a party and had a new long skirt made out of black and white Malaysian batik with a black, long-sleeved blouse. Local customs in dress were not as restrictive as they became later. Still, I didn't want to offend anyone with a low neckline, a sleeveless top, or a short skirt. And, so, we accepted the invitation.

When the evening came, it was quite exciting being around lots of people, who appeared to be among the upper crust of Kuantan society. Music played in the background as we mingled among men and women I had never met. Nate must have known a few, I can't remember. I do remember being awed by the grounds of the Sultan's palace. It was lovely, a great lawn laced around the edges with tropical flowers and foliage.

At some point, I noticed a long line of tables off to the side. Together they were probably fifty-feet long, covered in a series of tablecloths, with spoons, knives and plates marking short intervals. Soon a number of waiters dressed in long kain brought huge mounds of poached whole fish, large bowls of rice with side dishes, plus beef and chicken curries, and placed them on the tables. Soon we were summoned to come to the table to eat. We all found a place and stood to eat, as though we were a big extended family eating out of common bowls. If there was birthday cake afterwards, I don't remember it. It certainly would not have been traditional, as most Malaysians didn't eat fancy desserts after a meal. If they did, it was because the British colonials had introduced them.

Afterwards, there was dancing outside on the lawn. The Malay women looked lovely in their *baju kurung* and *kain.* The men were also wearing formal kain with shirts. Some of the kain were called *songket,* an elegant woven material that included designs in gold or silver threads. Nate and I danced, but we also watched as the Sultan monopolized the dance floor, asking a succession of women to dance with him. He was the featured dancer, a very tall, substantial man compared to most Malay men. You would have noticed him even if he had not been the Sultan. As he moved around the space, I hoped very much he would ask me to dance. It would have been something to brag to my children and grandchildren about. Alas, he did not ask.

I think it was only later that we learned about the fish we had for dinner. Nate thought it was probably carp. He heard that a certain root had been pounded into a kind of slurry by the Sultan's servants. Buckets of this were then thrown into the Pahang River upstream. This slurry apparently affected the nervous system of the fish and they died, floating on the surface of the water moving downstream. Men, women and children in the nearby villages were able to easily catch this enormous bounty of fish. They used their nets, or even their hands, to pull in fish after fish along the river's edge. Some fish were even part of the Sultan's birthday dinner, we assumed.

Nate and I were horrified by what we considered a blow to the Pahang River ecosystem. But we thought perhaps the Sultan did this to win favor with his constituents in the poorer villages. Or maybe as an appreciated gift from him. No doubt he succeeded. It was a cross-cultural situation which we had never encountered.

SIDE TRIP TO BURMA VIA BANGKOK

Out of the blue, Nate's parents announced they were traveling around the world, while we were still living in Malaysia. Nate's mother, the headmistress of a New England independent school, intended to visit alumnae in every country possible. Could we meet them in Bangkok? Although I was six months pregnant, we agreed. We also discovered that Burma would be opening to foreigners for a week starting in January of 1971, after a ten year closure. We were very curious to see that too.

To secure a local hotel and await their arrival, we went a day ahead to Bangkok. Nearly an hour away, the airport traffic demanded that we begin the trip there with time to spare. So we hired a taxi to meet them. Upon arrival, we noted that there were no planes on the tarmac and none scheduled. In fact, the airport was almost empty. After questioning the Pan Am agent we discovered that their daily flight had landed an hour early. We were shocked and didn't know what to do. Nate's parents had never been to

Thailand before—how were we ever going to find them? Luckily, we were directed to the airport message board where a note from Nate's father said: "We've gone to the Hilton Hotel. Hope to see you." Twelve thousand miles from home and he was hoping to see us. I couldn't imagine what we would have done if we hadn't seen that note.

So, we headed back to Bangkok and the Hilton: Nate's parents were in the lobby waiting in line for a room. As glad to see us as we were them, we urged them not to spend big money here, but to join us at our local hotel. Together we secured another taxi, stashed all their luggage, plus a large fur coat Nate's mother had brought to wear in Europe. Exhausted from the long journey, but also quite hungry, we introduced them to some Thai food in the hotel's little restaurant before we all headed to bed.

The next morning, Nate's parents both had to leave breakfast urgently, riding the elevator back to their room. Sick with stomach cramps, vomiting and diarrhea, they were not up for sight-seeing. We should have considered their unfamiliarity with Thai food and water. In a couple of days it was New Year's Eve but they still weren't ready to celebrate. So Nate and I left them to rest in their rooms that night, as we took off for the top floor of a new high-rise hotel, the Dusit Thani. The restaurant was luxurious, and because we had reservations, there were personalized matches ready at our table with Nate's name on them, Thai style: "Natebow Ditch."

In a few days, the senior Bowditches recovered and we could show them a bit of Bangkok. But they couldn't wait to find a Chinese restaurant, more familiar and less spicy to their palate. As for me, I was craving Mexican food. There were no Mexican restaurants in Malaysia, but there was one in Bangkok, and I insisted Nate take me there. Nate's mother gave me a look that said, if you were living in Asia, why would you want Mexican food? Maybe it was because I was pregnant, I wasn't sure. All I knew was that I thoroughly enjoyed some spicy enchiladas, tacos and burritos.

We introduced Nate's family to my family friends and godparents, Jim and Marj. Jim was working for USAID, based in Bangkok. They very graciously hosted us for a lovely American

During the Kingdom of Pagan, Burma, more than 10,000 Buddhist temples were built across a plain between the 11th and 13th century. This is a view of what remained in 1971.

dinner. Afterwards, since we were about to depart for Burma, they kept most of Nate's parents' luggage, including the fur coat. They would collect everything on the return to Bangkok.

After a couple of hours in the air, we landed into what was then called Rangoon. Like Thailand, it was also a Buddhist country, but the temples were different: huge bell shaped structures, covered in gold leaf. The Thai temples had layered roofs, with delicate uplifted edges to ward off evil spirits, but lots of gold leaf as well. Rangoon seemed a lovely, if slightly rundown, capital that hadn't been open to foreigners for more than a day since 1962. To make it easier for

Nate's parents, we reserved two adjoining rooms at The Strand, an old British colonial hotel. They loved it and I had to admit it had a certain panache. I enjoyed the quiet atmosphere, off of busy streets, as well as the old British standards in the bar and in the food. I always had an attraction/repulsion toward the British as colonial powers in Asia. I had read a lot of Somerset Maugham's stories, especially those in which the British were caught off-guard cross-culturally. Of course, the same thing happened to many Americans traveling abroad in more recent times. This included me.

In any case, we enjoyed The Strand before flying up to Pagan, with its ancient temples, and an old British Rest House. We had stayed in old British Rest Houses before, but this one was barely acceptable. I had to give Nate's parents credit for not complaining about bathrooms and bed linens that looked like they had never been cleaned. Also, the toilets were the kind you stood over, something I knew they had never used. But somehow, we all managed.

Thousands of ancient Buddhist temples filled the plain around Pagan. We learned that Pagan was founded in the second century AD, but the ancient temples were from the ninth to the thirteenth centuries when Pagan became a huge Kingdom. Even pregnant, I climbed to the top of some. It was visually mind-blowing. We walked into several interiors, many with Buddhas carved into the walls. At one, we seemed to have surprised a young Burmese man, who looked like he was cutting small Buddha statues away from the wall and collecting them in a pile. He offered us two small ones, as if afraid of being caught should we inform the authorities. In retrospect there was no doubt we shouldn't have accepted them, but we did.

We headed to Mandalay next, perhaps more because of the old movie called *On the Road to Mandalay*. It was much less interesting than Pagan, but we enjoyed walking around the quiet town, into street markets, and in large parks with banyan trees. Both the men and the women wore *longyis* tied around their waists like sarongs. We also tried a little Burmese food, including *Khow suey*, a relatively mild, but flavorful, soup, which we all loved. We then flew back to Rangoon for one more night.

After another stay at The Strand, we prepared to return to Malaysia via Bangkok, with Nate's parents. It was only after our plane had taken off that we opened the national newspaper and read an article that said, as of that day, no antique artifacts would be allowed out of the country. It was too late.

To The Pacific

The author having a laugh and warm hug with Ate outside the bahay kubo, behind their home in Malolos, Bulacan, the Philippines, 1972.

THE PHILIPPINES, PAPUA NEW GUINEA
AND NEW ZEALAND

In April of 1972, it was time to leave Malaysia and we had to sell my little MG. We put an ad in The Straits Times newspaper and a bidding war erupted between Bangkok and Singapore. We ended up selling it for ten times our purchase price. This enabled us to fly off to the Pacific Islands, with one-year-old Windi in tow, en route back to the United States. It had been a wonderful three years and we vowed we would do it again, as soon as another opportunity presented itself.

We decided it would be best for all three of us to go home via

Kuya playing with Windi during a visit to the home of my Filipino family in Malolos, Bulacan, the Philippines, 1972.

Nate and I visited the home of my godson Elmer and his father in Malolos, Bulacan, the Philippines, 1969.

the Pacific, instead of through Europe. Since we had chosen Maine as our destination, both ways were just about equally long, but the Pacific would be more laid back, we assumed, and we could visit people we knew along the way. We had the money from the sale of the MG, three plane tickets, and no job ahead. But Nate had been admitted to Princeton for his graduate work, and they would pay for his tuition and housing for two years. We were lucky.

We flew to the Philippines to introduce our daughter, Windi, to my Filipino family. They all loved holding and playing with her. Windi was used to a lot of people. In Malaysia she saw Volunteers and other staff regularly. We were lucky here too, since she wasn't afraid of strangers. In Malolos we also introduced her to the family of my godson, Elmer. He was still a little boy then, so he probably didn't remember meeting her.

When we left for Papua New Guinea, we were advised by the Peace Corps doctor to give Windi a sedative for the long flight, which started at midnight, lasting for more than six hours. Unfortunately, Windi was practically jumping off the ceiling of the plane during the whole flight. She slept not at all. Constantly apologizing to the annoyed passengers around us, it didn't help that we didn't get any sleep either. We learned too late that sometimes sedatives for children had the opposite effect. But at last, we arrived in Port Moresby in the morning, found a guest house and slept for most of the day. When we awakened we were famished. We found a little place that sold fried fish and chips wrapped in a newspaper.

I had never had fish and chips before, but they were scrumptious.

Part of Melanesia, the island of New Guinea was split between Indonesia and Australia. The Eastern half was called Papua, New Guinea, and at the time a territory of Australia. The island intrigued me because of the unique and fine craftsmanship of the different ethnic groups in the interior. I had originally hoped we could take Windi down the Sepik River to visit the people there. But others discouraged me from doing that because of the risk to Windi, far from doctors, and through lots of mosquitoes, without protection. I was disappointed, but I agreed, finally.

Instead we decided to fly up to Goroka in the mountains, because something called the Sing Sing was going to happen there during our visit. I wasn't really clear what a Sing Sing was but it sounded interesting, so we flew up in a transport plane, buckled into seats along its sides. We even made a stop on a mountain along the way, and I couldn't help but chuckle at a small wooden shack on the runway with a huge sign that said "International Airport."

Unbeknown to us, among the passengers was a missionary

The author with sleeping Windi, flying to Goroka in a cargo plane from Port Moresby to the Sing-Sing in Goroka, Papua, New Guinea, 1972.

Windi with a new acquaintance in Goroka, Papua New Guinea, where we were visiting the Sing Sing, a meeting of different ethnic groups, 1972.

couple. They introduced themselves and invited us to stay with them. We took them up on their offer, since we had no idea where to stay in Goroka. The man of the family was kind to us and held Windi during dinner so that we could eat, without worrying about her. We felt very welcome.

The next day was the Sing Sing. If I interpreted it correctly, it was an opportunity for all the different ethnic groups in Papua New Guinea to come together, to celebrate by creatively dressing, as they sang and danced. I didn't know much of the history of the event, but I had heard that many groups were fearful of each other, having fought each other in past local wars. I could see that some walked around in a wary fashion. From another perspective it was also a market for exchanging goods and for marriage contracts, I learned. In other words for some, attracting wealth and women set the priorities.

At one point our daughter, walking around with us, encountered a youngster just about her age, and yet so different. Windi reached out to her to touch her necklace of seeds. After the Sing Sing was over, most of the individuals who were in face paint, cast off their

The author at the Sing Sing in Goroka, Papua New Guinea, with an individual wonderfully decked-out in feathers, tusks and shells—drinking a Coca Cola, 1972. (photo with permission)

Windi and Nate looking out upon the ocean, on a beach in Vanuatu, New Hebrides, 1972.

costumes made from shells, feathers, leaves, vines, seeds, pigs tusks, and bark. I couldn't help but pick up one of the discarded belts created from these natural materials. I took it with me as a remembrance.

The only other souvenir we collected was an Iatmul mask in Port Moresby at a gallery. The Iatmul people lived along the Sepik River, one of the largest populations on the river where we had hoped to go. Instead, this mask substituted for the experience. I was enamored with the designs and materials, even though it cost us a precious thirty-five US dollars. Only our second investment in art, we had purchased a beautiful batik painting in Malaysia by Khalil Ibrahim, depicting Malay fishermen and women gathering in their nets after fishing. Meanwhile, we had the wonderful mask shipped home, and soon we were on our way again.

Unfortunately, I didn't keep a diary during this trip, too busy looking out for fast-walking one-year-old, Windi, I imagine. So, to be honest, but sadly, the Solomon Islands, the New Hebrides and New Caledonia have all run together and faded for me. I remember a simple way of life, and a beach for Windi near Honiara in the Solomons, finding a WWII airplane underwater near Vanuatu, in the New Hebrides, as well as the very expensive city of Noumea in New Caledonia. But, most significantly, I remember facing, for the first time, our inability to find disposable diapers.

New Zealand became the saving grace in the diaper category. We stocked up as many Pampers as we could in our combined luggage. Windi's small suitcase became mostly diapers, stuffed inside. But New Zealand turned out to be a lifesaver in other ways too. We spent most of our time on the South Island because we knew we would see beaches as well as a glacier. We rented a car very inexpensively, and bought fresh veggies, meat, and milk, on a daily basis. The bottles cost more than the milk, so we kept turning them in at grocery stores along the way. We kept everything in the boot of our car because it was like a refrigerator in there. When we arrived at a cheap motel with a kitchenette we were all set for the evening.

It turned out to be winter when we arrived in New Zealand. I don't know if I had really thought that one through. Still, we

Windi taking a bath in the motel kitchen sink in South Island, New Zealand, 1972.

could buy some second-hand warm clothes for Windi, and a couple of jackets for us at a thrift shop. We traveled around the island from Christchurch to Mount Cook, to the glacier on the coast, and back. I had never seen a glacier so close to the ocean. When we walked the quarter mile to see it up close and touch it, it was staggeringly cold and extended probably twenty feet above our heads. We suddenly noticed that Windi was turning a little blue. We knew we had to return to the beach right away. She regained her color, but it was certainly a highlight to see a glacier up close and personal. We also delighted in the color of the water as it cascaded down Mount Cook and ran joyfully through the rivers. The water was a turquoise color I had never seen before. I heard it had something to do with the copper in the rocks.

We did spend a little time on the North Island, mainly to get a sense of the Maori culture and traditions. I was especially interested in their designs. We were able to visit an outdoor program for tourists, which was less than ideal. This was really all we had time for, other than to learn what we could of the Maori in a history museum in Wellington. It turns out that more than one thousand years ago, waves of Polynesian migrations, originally from Tahiti ended up in New Zealand, the ancestors of the Maori people.

In a few days we were off to Fiji, Windi and her diapers in tow.

FIJI, THE SAMOAS, TAHITI AND MOOREA

We had heard that in Fiji there was a wonderful boat trip in the Asawa Islands. I had forgotten that I would probably be seasick on the ocean, but we landed in Suva, Fiji, with that boat trip already purchased.

Fortunately, for me, we flew to one of the Asawa islands, and then began our sailing through various smaller islands on a gorgeous transparent calm sea. There was another group of maybe ten or so people on board. Considering it was a small yacht, we were given a tiny room under the top deck with two single beds and a playpen squeezed between them. Somehow we made it work. Windi slept like a log on the rolling boat, and we knew she would be safe there. And I managed not to get seasick.

We were touched with how the crew handled Windi for us, tossing her gently from staff person to staff person, from the

The author and daughter, Windi, with a flower head lei, on the boat we traveled among the Asawa Islands, Fiji. I was blissfully not experiencing any nausea on the water because it was so calm, 1972.

sailboat to the shore, at each landing, that we happily encouraged it. That meant we didn't have to carry her across the surf. Windi, by now, had learned not to eat the sand on the beach, and loved running up and down and splashing her feet in the water, a big smile on her face, laughing. This made it a paradise for all of us. And the cuisine that the chef created was amazing. Fresh seafood, of course—shrimp and fish, plus tender steaks, lots of fresh vegetables, papaya and mangoes were a treat at sea.

Unfortunately, we didn't have much opportunity to explore the rest of Fiji. Our short time in the capital of Suva was almost disrespectful. I did note that the Fijians were strong and statuesque; also noted the presence of many Indians, who seemed to control the businesses. We were quickly on our way to Western Samoa. An American friend from Malaysia, Michael was now Peace Corps Director there. Upon arrival, we learned that the wife of one of his PCVS had just that week swam out to the edge of a reef and been eaten by a shark. It seemed almost unbelievable that this could happen. I felt for her husband and her family at home, hearing

Windi enjoying some time with the generous and kind Samoan family whom we visited at their home on the water in Western Samoa. They suggested we nap while they took care of her, and we slept on mats on a bamboo floor, 1972.

The Samoan woman outside her oceanside home, where we visited her in Western Samoa in 1972.

this devastating news. I also felt for Michael, having to deal with this tragic situation.

Michael's house reflected his creativity in incorporating Samoan crafts and arts as interior decoration. I loved the huge, somewhat broken pots arranged artfully outside his entryway. There were tapa cloths on the wall and sculpture carefully placed for viewing. I especially loved the stunning, carved wooden fishing tackle box on his table, and I remarked to Michael on it. He said it was from Tonga and that I should take it, if I agreed to do a favor for him. When we returned to the States, he wanted me to order some drapery rods from Sears and have them sent to him in Samoa. Of course I agreed—more than a fair trade for me.

Before our departure from Malaysia, the new Peace Corps director there heard we were including Western Samoa in our travels. As the former director, he and his family had become good friends with a delightful Samoan family on the opposite side of the island from the capital. He contacted them to say we would like to spend a day with them. As we arrived along the southern coast, and introduced ourselves, a magnificent day greeted us, beautiful in every respect. The skies were an aqua color, shot through with an assortment of clouds. The day was warm, but the breeze was cooling. This family humbly exuded graciousness, generosity and gentleness as they welcomed us. Their home's open floor plan, embraced by bamboo and thatch, rested right on the ocean. The waves practically lapped at their house poles. The husband was a fisherman, and he roasted us the most delicious fish I had ever eaten, fresh and crunchy. Afterwards, the wife told us to go rest while they would look after Windi. We complied willingly, lying atop fine mats on the bamboo floor, falling asleep, covered by the afternoon's light breeze.

Moving on to Pago Pago, American Samoa, we found it difficult to enjoy, as the rain pounded on the island the whole time we were there. I remember lying in my bed at The Rainmaker Hotel, reading. The story: Somerset Maugham's "Rain," had actually been written in Pago Pago. I felt I was living it too. After a couple of wet days, we prepared to embark on the last stretch of our journey through the Pacific, to Tahiti in Polynesia.

Tahiti looked exotic, as Gauguin might have imagined it when he lived there. The landscape was beautiful, but the capital of Papeete, struck us as extraordinarily expensive compared to most of the places we had traveled. We could barely afford the hotel, much less the French food served in restaurants. The women, dressed in bright floral cottons, reminded me of muumuus in Hawaii.

After renting a car and driving around the island for a few days, we felt we needed to look at another island. We chose Moorea because it wasn't far, though we would need to take a ferry, crossing over some rough seas to get there. I wasn't excited about that, but I fought the nausea, looking straight ahead, talking to no one, while Nate held Windi. I made it in one piece, but barely.

On arrival, we weren't sure where to go. The nearest populated place was, of all things, a Club Med on the shore. This wasn't my kind of place, but I gave in when we found we could buy chits for drinks and food, and let Windi play along the water. The weather was hot and dry, not ideal for traipsing around the island. In the meantime, Windi had a great time, picking up shells, running in and out of the water, while we relaxed on beach chairs, one eye each on her.

When time came to ferry back to Papeete, I said I just didn't think I could endure another rocky boat ride. We checked in with Club Med and discovered there was a flight I could take, thirty minutes in the air from Moorea to Papeete. We could ill afford it, but I had to hand it to Nate, he said okay. I flew and he ferried back with Windi. We got back about the same time.

Since we were running out of money after nearly two months in the Pacific, it was time to book our flight to Honolulu. Another long daytime flight must have gone well since I recall none of it. Our arrival in the late afternoon one early summer day, led us into the open arms of my parents. They were hugging their first grandchild. And we had just a couple of disposable diapers left. Good timing.

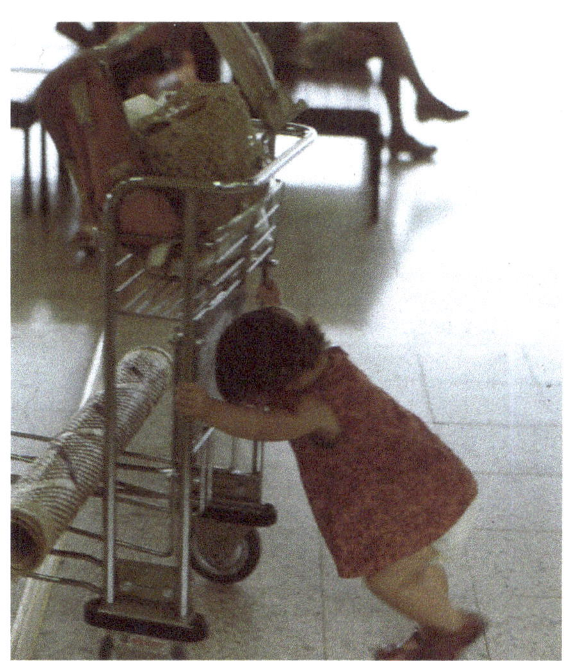

Windi pushing our luggage cart at the Honolulu airport, upon our arrival there. Traveling home from Malaysia, 1972.

Reuniting with the author's family on the beach at Hanauma Bay, near Honolulu, Hawaii, 1972.

Windi and her grandfather, in matching swimsuits, walking together for the first time, in the ocean off of Honolulu, Hawaii, en route home from Malaysia, 1972.

SRI LANKA

The entire family—the author, Windi, Sean and Nate—waiting at the Portland, Maine airport to take off for three years in Sri Lanka, 1983.

COLOMBO, SRI LANKA

On the last leg of our journey to Sri Lanka, I couldn't understand why the woman in front of me was carrying a plastic dish drainer in 1983. Weren't those available in Colombo? I would soon find out when we completed the journey to our new destination.

Starting in Maine a few weeks earlier, we flew the first leg overseas from Honolulu, via Japan, to an overnight in Hong Kong, and another one in Bangkok. We were all exhausted when we collapsed in our room following our arrival at Hong Kong's terrifying Kai Tak airport. We had Windi, twelve, and Sean, seven, with us for this next adventure. Sean, completely jet lagged, woke up in the middle of the night starving. Luckily, I had saved some crackers and cheese from the last flight. In Bangkok the next day, both kids were amazed to hear their father speak Thai to the taxi driver at the airport. This was new for them, as was sitting on the floor of the restaurant in a Bangkok hotel trying out Thai food.

Finally, we were in Colombo. The ride into town took more than an hour, but the beautiful old traditional hotel named the Galle Face, was waiting for us. The columns on the terrace housed singing birds in their capitols. Orchids graced the lobby as we checked in. Encircling its own grounds, the hotel kept the surrounding noise and chaos of city streets at bay. The interior gardens appeared to be edged by the crashing surf of the Indian Ocean (despite an invisible train track between them), and included a salt water pool and three different restaurants. This is where we would stay until we found a house in which to live.

Our first cultural issue came from Sean who had never tasted curries before, and nothing as hot as Sri Lankan food. Based on my experience of curries, it was the hottest I had ever eaten. Nate and I enjoyed them, but they certainly made our faces red, sweat dripping down our foreheads. All Sean wanted was an American hamburger, but all hamburgers proved to be spiced with hot chilies. He would lay his head in my lap and cry, so we went to every hotel restaurant we could find looking for non-spicy hamburgers, but to no avail. Breads and cereal it was, with peanut butter and some tropical fruit thrown in.

This time Nate had a direct services contract with USAID. He was going to help start a Sri Lankan Business Development Center with a local colleague. For the first time living overseas, we were given some luxury: a house provided with what appeared to be Drexel brand furniture, re-upholstering costs covered by USAID, plus carpets, even a washer and a dryer. We also had the use of the American Embassy commissary, the help of the Embassy travel agency, and the Embassy nurse's medical assistance. Our home was in a part of Colombo called Cinnamon Gardens, evoking a fragrant trading past. Compared to our past lives in other countries, this was an upgrade. Never mind that someone cut the low sloping telephone line to our house every other day, looking for copper wire, but the phone company religiously replaced it every time. This was nothing like our life in Malaysia, but we were still determined to pursue cultural experiences and friendship among the Sri Lankans.

Our daughter, Windi, had sobbed when she first learned that we were heading to Sri Lanka. She would have to leave her Middle School friends and her dog, Firecracker, behind. I was saddened by her reaction, but told her that we would all go through this new adventure together. As for Sean, as long as he was with us, and didn't have to eat spicy hamburgers, he would be fine.

Both kids attended The Colombo Overseas Children's School, designed mostly for expatriates from different countries, but many Sri Lankans were starting to attend as well. I even became a temporary school admissions counsellor for awhile. Six months had passed when Windi confessed to me that being here was the best thing that had ever happened to her. I was somewhat flabbergasted,

Sean and his Sri Lankan best friend, Chandeep, visiting us in Maine, 1988, while bringing his sister, Dinusha, to college at Farmington, Maine.

Windi and her best Sri Lankan friend, Dinusha, visiting us in Maine, in 1988, just before she started college at the University of Maine in Farmington.

but she explained that it was due to the friends she had made from all over the world, from places she had never heard of before. I also figured out that, even more importantly, since most expatriates left after two to three years, it was hard for cliques to form. Everyone seemed to make the most of their time together with new friends. She regularly hung out with kids from Germany, the Philippines, the Netherlands, Malaysia, and, of course, Sri Lanka.

Our great fortune came when we were introduced to Chandra and Indira. They had two children, Dinusha and Chandeep, who were almost the same age as our two. We spent a lot of time with this family, visiting their little weekend house on stilts near the ocean in Negombo, staying in a guest house in the cool mountains around Bandarawela, visiting Yala National Park together, enjoying wonderful times on the beach, and at historic monuments. We became best friends as a family, and as individuals.

Indira was born into a family, who were originally money lenders from southern India. Although her parents wouldn't allow her to attend law school, she studied her brother's law texts instead. The father of her husband, Chandra, became the first Ambassador to the US from Ceylon. Chandra's childhood was therefore partly in America where he grew to love jazz, among other things American. In Sri Lanka he was a senior tea taster for Lipton Tea Company, although he preferred coffee. So they both came from privileged backgrounds but were exceedingly humble and kind.

Sri Lanka, itself, had a fascinating story. The island, located in the Indian Ocean, was first discovered by the Arabs, who called it Serendib—an unexpected discovery—the origin of our word "serendipity." The Greeks called it Taprobane, but the countries that colonized it had their own names: Ceilao by the Portuguese, Ceylan by the Dutch, and Ceylon by the British. Each of those countries left their mark: Christianity was brought by the Portuguese priests, business and trade by the Dutch traders, and government and education by the British colonizers. Upon Independence, Ceylon changed its name to Sri Lanka, meaning "resplendent isle," suiting it perfectly. The mixture of European and Asian influences helped make Sri Lanka very sophisticated cross-culturally—at least in the big cities. It was interesting to note that most all the women there dressed in full-length sarees from India.

We were told that there had been historical resentment between the Sinhalese and the Tamils within the country. We saw some of it when many Tamils we first met, fled as a war between the two ethnic groups began festering in the north. It seemed that the Sinhalese had been generally overlooked by the British, choosing Tamils more often to be in government positions. Now the Sinhalese were in charge. They had been the first migrants to the island, originally descended from northern Indians, and were responsible for bringing Buddhism here. It was said that the tooth of the Buddha was stored secretly in Kandy, the Sinhalese Buddhist capital of the country.

This combination of Sri Lanka's heritage, new friends, travel around a gorgeous island country, its hills carpeted in green tea plantations, developed into a special time for our family. The names flowed off our tongues: Jayawardene, Dissanayake, Jayatilleka, Kollupitiya, Nuwara Eliya. We studied Sinhalese together; attended local cultural concerts and plays; organized a cross-cultural women's group; bought inexpensive sprays of orchids every week; looked at sapphires and rubies with our friend Siri; bought brass buckets and artifacts from a trader; and frequented a shop called Barefoot for weavings by unwed mothers. We also learned to eat festive savory *lamprais,* as well as *kiribath, pittu, papadams, stringhoppers, watalappam, plus the* Indian *masala thosai, and mulligatawny,* all milder examples of the delicious South Asian cuisine. Once in a while we even baked a European influenced *Love Cake.*

We enjoyed many dinner invitations with our friends, both formal and casual. Many Asians, including Sri Lankans, ate with their hands. When I confessed to Indira that I didn't like using my hands to eat because it felt unclean, she replied: we always know that our hands are clean, but we never know whether the silverware is, given how many others have used them when eating. The other interesting cross-cultural issue in dining with friends, was that drinking and tasting '*short eats*' typically lasted from about eight until about eleven in the evening. Then dinner was served.

With Sri Lankan friends on an excursion to an ancient water tank in Sri Lanka. Sunita and Heather, Lalith and Preethi, Indira and Chandra, the author and Nate, plus all of the combined children.

Everyone ate quickly, and said their goodbyes. In other words, the Sri Lankans liked to extend the evening as long as possible before eating dinner. This was difficult for us to reconcile with our eating habits, which were almost the opposite.

We really valued our Sri Lankan life, so it was very difficult for each of us to leave. Indira, Chandra and their family joined us at our hotel on the last night. Indira waited until then to ask why we did not go to church or practice Christianity. I didn't have a good answer for her. Meanwhile, Nate and all the kids took off to climb Adam's Peak together, an overnight expedition. The next day, both families tried to continue the experience until the very last minute. We finally hugged Indira, Chandra, Dinusha and Chandeep, in a tearful farewell.

An hour later, waiting at the airport, I suddenly remembered that I had never found a dish drainer in this country and learned to live without one.

Susan Wilson Bowditch

SLEEPING AROUND SRI LANKA

During our first couple of years of living in the capital city of Sri Lanka, we drove to many old cultural sites. While ancient Greeks were enjoying their prime time, Anuradhapura was the seat of a civilization too. The sacred Bodhi tree made it especially interesting, still growing after nearly twenty-three centuries, according to legend. I learned that Buddha had gained enlightenment under this tree in India. Legend also has it that a sapling was later carried surreptitiously from there to this island country. It seemed to have survived under continuous management by a long succession of caretakers and grew to be a great sized tree with enormous limbs. Metal supports were put under the branches some time ago, and at one point a botanical expert from America's Smithsonian treated it so it would continue to survive. We enjoyed viewing the tree from our simple guest house—when not visited by a tribe of monkeys hoping for handouts.

Polonnaruwa was not as ancient, but full of the ruins of old capital buildings. There we stayed in a guest house that had been created for Queen Elizabeth and Prince Philip who stayed there

Windi, with a monkey on her shoulder in Anuradhapura, looking for nits in her hair, 1985.

during a visit to Ceylon in 1954. Not quite as spiffy when we were there, it was a comfortable place to take in the sites. Of most interest to me was the lovely bath, created in stone tiers of lotus flower petals where once water cascaded. The kids loved the forty-six foot long reclining Buddha carved from a single piece of granite, his head resting on a slightly dented stone pillow.

But the most fascinating of all had to be Sigiriya. The story progressed as if reading an ancient murder novel. Fifteen centuries ago the oldest son of a king had a commoner for a mother. His younger brother's mother was of royalty. Thus the elder son greatly feared that he would be pushed out of the royal succession. To avoid that possibility, he walled his father alive within a tomb, and proceeded to build a palace atop a 600-foot stone monolith, claiming himself king. His brother fled to India as a result. Created for the new king were pools, gardens, and paintings of beautiful bare-breasted young women, just for his enjoyment. Eventually his younger brother returned with an army, and

Sigiriya, a six-hundred-foot-high monolith, became the fortress of a prince who usurped his father, the king, by walling him alive inside a tomb. Originally Sigiriya had a giant sculpted lion entrance, now only the paws exist. Late 5th century.

at some point during the confrontation, the king cut his own throat with his dagger and put it back in its sheath before dying, according to our guide.

It was still possible to climb to the top of Sigiriya. In the old days people had climbed through a giant crouching stone lion, then pulled themselves up to the top on notches in the huge rock. On this day, only the astonishing paws of the lion entrance still existed, but after that there were railings to help pull one up. As each of us passed through the Mirror Wall, we could still see the lovely remains of several paintings. At the top of the rock was a magnificent view of gardens below and beyond, well worth the difficult climb.

We had other wonderful trips in Sri Lanka. Once we visited the whales who came to breed off of the eastern coastal town of Trincomolee. Another time we rented a big fishing boat that went on the Indian Ocean, but which I made return to shore because I was seasick. I could hear the locals, speaking in Sinhalese, laughing at me, the crazy white woman, as we came ashore. We stayed in hotels and camped with Sri Lankan friends on the coast below Colombo. We stayed in the cool highlands among tea plantations near Nuwara Eliya. We drove to the cold Horton Plains so Nate could fish for trout, and at nearby World's End where we could have a fine view over the country. It had a vertical drop of one mile over an escarpment. We heard that many star-crossed lovers had lost their lives there. On our last night in Colombo, Nate and the kids climbed all night to the top of famous Adam's peak which makes a near perfect triangular shadow at sunrise. But best of all we stayed in the national parks.

Wilpattu was in the deep jungle. We had rented a rather large bungalow in the park, without electricity, but with a broad open veranda and four beds covered by mosquito nets, plus an inside bedroom for Nate's visiting parents. The rest of us slept on the veranda, waking up frequently to the multiple sounds of the jungle. Contrary to popular opinion, jungles could be very loud, especially at night. It was such a thrill to actually be there. Our daytime outlook was for a bear or a leopard. It was only as we finally drove out that we spotted a leopard asleep in a tree, and a bear that crossed the road behind us.

Yala (Ruhunga) National Park, on the other hand, was very dry and lacking in significant vegetation. Nearer a beautiful empty beach on the south side of the island nation, we rented an even simpler bungalow, lacking both electricity and beds, along with a couple of other Sri Lankan families. We all had a good time swimming in the ocean, then cooking in the rudimentary kitchen, and finally bedding down for the night in our sarongs on mats lined up on the floor. We had hoped to see a leopard at the park, but we failed. In the morning, however, one of our group noticed that his leather slippers, which had been left just outside the half door, had been ripped to pieces. A leopard had definitely connected with our bungalow sometime during the night.

FAMILY TRIP TO THAILAND

During spring break in Colombo, Sri Lanka, we decided to take off for nearby Thailand, where Nate had served as a Peace Corps Volunteer. He had lived in the far south in Yala, working with physical education teachers integrating new ideas for their respective schools. Yala was south, near the Malaysian border, but we were headed to Bangkok and places north. After a short flight and a long taxi ride, we were soon settled in a room with four beds at the YWCA in Bangkok. The daily oatmeal got a little tiresome, but otherwise it was a clean safe place to stay. Our intent was to introduce our kids to Thailand, which we had both loved.

One day we all took a taxi to the Thai Physical Education Department, with the hope that Nate might meet his former co-worker, Samart. It had been sixteen years since they had seen each other. Unfortunately, the office said that Samart was up north in Udon Thani province. So, Nate left him a message and the phone number at the YWCA, just in case he returned while we were there.

We spent the afternoon visiting temples, floating in a boat on the Chao Phraya River, eating street food, and meeting the very friendly Thais. Since Nate was fluent in Thai, he made it easy for the rest of us. Occasionally a young man wanted to know how old our twelve-year-old daughter was. She enjoyed the fact that these handsome young men appeared interested in her. In the process she learned how to say her age, *sip saawng*, which sounded like "sip song".

After we returned to the Y to rest in the heat of the mid-afternoon, a staff person knocked on our door to say that there was a phone call for Nate. He got up quickly to take the call. Much to his surprise, it was Samart, who had just gotten back from Udon a few minutes ago. He asked to meet us at a certain restaurant at five p.m. and Nate agreed.

At nearly five our taxi pulled up at the restaurant. As we got out, Nate hugged Samart, then introduced each of us in turn: first me, then Windi, and finally Sean. I could see that Samart was nearly in tears meeting the family of his co-worker for the first time. This significant moment brought me to tears as well. In a few moments we were seated at a round table outside, with Thai music blaring in the background.

While Nate and Samart caught up in Thai, I helped the kids order Thai food they would enjoy, avoiding the heat of Sri Lankan dishes. Amazingly—to both of them—a waiter stood behind each of their chairs with a large bottle of Coca Cola in hand. As soon as Sean or Windi drank half of their Coke, the waiter topped it up. They obviously loved every minute of this routine, despite my threatening glances, since we did not keep Coke available at home. I also delighted in seeing Nate so happy reconnecting with his old co-worker, talking Thai again. What an evening.

The next day we bought train tickets to Chiang Mai in the north. It was an overnight train so we got on in the early evening, settling into four bunks opposite each other. We had brought fruit, nuts and drinks with us as the train didn't serve dinner. It turned out to be an interesting evening when Sean climbed into his father's bunk and pulled the privacy curtain. The next thing Windi and I heard was incredulous laughing from Sean. Asking his father how babies were conceived explained the loud laughter from an eight-year-old, we later learned.

Nate's Peace Corps physical education colleague, Samart, with his wife, in Yala, Thailand, 1966. The author's entire family had the unexpected opportunity to meet Samart in Bangkok in 1984. It was a special moment.

We awoke to a bright morning in Chiang Mai. The small city was known for its fine handicrafts. An active night market provided us with an exciting experience as well as delicious food to try. A youthful atmosphere pervaded Chiang Mai, making it a fun place to visit. But our plan was to travel even farther north, to visit one of the Hill Tribes with a guide. The various Hill Tribes had moved down from China to Burma, Thailand and Laos, over many years. They were very distinct in their separate languages, dress and cultures, compared to each other and the countries where they settled.

After a few days, we got in a truck heading toward Chiang Rai. There were several other visitors joining us on benches opposite each other. Following a bumpy ride of a couple of hours, we got down and hiked a few miles to one of the villages of the Akha ethnic group. There we learned about how they created their adornments of silver jewelry, clothing, and footwear. Then we watched them cook and helped in the preparation. Finally, as night fell, we were led to a bamboo platform, lined with rows of sleeping pads and blankets, under a thatched roof.

Ours was the only family of four. It was a cold night, but most of us slept heavily after a long day of trekking. Suddenly, in the night we heard a man calling out to someone in French, and a boy crying. It turned out that Sean had slept-walked over to the wrong person, thinking it was his father. The man in question was a Frenchman who scarcely understood what was happening. We calmed both down, brought Sean back to our sleeping area and returned to sleep.

In the morning we were invited to ride elephants, an enticing way out of the Akha land, but Sean was understandably scared. Instead we walked again in the humid air and hot sunshine for the few miles. By the time we reached the road, I was soaked to the skin. So I stood behind a big sign and wrapped myself in a sarong, shedding my clothes underneath. Soon a truck came along to pick us up. Unfortunately, the truck had only a front seat with the driver. But all four of us squeezed in together, kids on our laps, Nate sitting with the gear shift between his legs. It was another long and bumpy ride back to Chiang Mai, but no one complained. The next day we got back on the train to Bangkok. In a few days we were in Colombo again, all of us grateful that Thailand had been, even momentarily, in our lives.

TRAVELING HOME
FROM SRI LANKA

An example of a fully decked-out jeepney, the main form of public transportation in the Philippines, 1986.

SINGAPORE AND MALAYSIA

When we departed Sri Lanka, I spontaneously kissed the airport tarmac, expressing farewell to a memorable experience. Because the departure affected our whole family, it seemed unusually emotional. We were all sad. But soon our night flight to Singapore led us to another Y, four beds in a row. We slept like we had never slept before. Meanwhile, each of us had one backpack to carry. Whatever we needed for clothes was stuffed in there, enough for at least a week. We charged our now ten-year-old son and fifteen-year-old daughter, to be responsible for their clothes and other belongings. We were not interested in spending a lot of money getting clothes washed and ironed on this trip. Also, if they wanted to buy any new clothes or souvenirs, they would need to get rid of something in their pack. Actually, that plan worked fairly well, all things considered. Of course, we did have to get some laundry done more than once on a journey of two months.

As exhausted as we seemed, everyone was game to rush off to Burger King for breakfast the next morning. Time to have some junk food. We missed breakfast, but had Whoppers instead. Taking the afternoon to walk around a new Singapore along old Orchard Road, I thought everything looked so much taller and wealthier than the one we had encountered fourteen years ago. Beethoven's Record Shop was still there, but the Malaysian Hotel with the beautiful batik mural by Malaysian artist Seah Kim Joo was gone. Nate and I fondly recalled meeting an older Chinese gentleman on the street back then, grilling giant shrimp for sale. We bought some and found it to be the tastiest we had ever eaten. I even asked for his "recipe" so that I could replicate it one day. He said his story

Sarasa and Bala at home in Penang, our good friends in Kuantan, Pahang, Malaysia, when we lived there, 1986. We are still in touch.

was that he had actually been a rich man before the war but had lost everything when the Japanese occupied Singapore. We didn't know whether it was true or not, but we chose to believe it.

To get another perspective on things, we headed to the old Raffles Hotel, named after Britain's Sir Stanford Raffles, celebrating its one-hundredth anniversary. Many famous writers had slept and written here: Somerset Maugham, James Michener, Rudyard Kipling, and Joseph Conrad to name a few. Known for its Singapore Sling, the drink was created by a Chinese bartender during British Colonial times. We didn't imbibe, but crossed the street in the growing dusk, to a big open park. Filled with many food kiosks, we could take our pick, mix and match among any of them, and eat at a table in the park. We tried a bit of everything, but the kids especially loved the spicy, but not too hot, satay on sticks.

The next day we flew up to Penang, Malaysia, where we reunited with our Malaysian Indian friends, Sarasa and Bala, and introduced Sean and our nearly grown daughter. Their children were grown too, and I thought that Windi took a liking to one of their boys, seventeen-year-old Vijay. Perhaps as a mild alert, Sarasa told us she

The Raffles Hotel in Singapore, famous for its Singapore Sling drink, seen during our visit there en route home from Sri Lanka, 1986.

would soon be looking for good marriage partners for her sons. She also admitted that she might not have the opportunity to decide this. But, she said she had warned her sons against marrying interculturally or interracially. She felt less concerned by Malaysians who were Chinese or Malay, since they experienced the same national culture. Our reunion continued by filling us with good conversation, warmth, and food from the Kashmiri Restaurant, which included Tandoori chicken, Nepalese curries, sweet sesame naan and paratha.

While there, we were looking forward to finding the parents of Boon, the student we hosted from Bates College. Nate had officiated at Boon's wedding to Beth. While Windi walked down the aisle as the flower girl, Sean, Nate and I, acting on his parents' behalf, walked Boon down the aisle. When we finally met Boon's parents, we took to them immediately, and celebrated our friendship with their son, by taking them to Kentucky Fried Chicken for lunch, partly to appease our kids, as well as to introduce Boon's parents to someplace they had never eaten.

According to Boon's father, many people in Malaysia had had

The father of Boon, the Bates College student we hosted in Maine in the 1970's, with Sean, when we visited him and his wife, in Penang, Malaysia, 1986.

enough of Malay preference, meaning the land, and some other privileges belonging to the Malays, the *Bumiputera,* ostensibly being in the land first. He said that now that the country had achieved a higher standard of living he thought it would eventually end. But Indian and Chinese Malaysians seemed powerless to stop it. They resented the government's aggressive policies, giving Malays priority for higher education, jobs, even government scholarships abroad. It reminded me somewhat of the Sinhalese and Tamil situation we had just left in Sri Lanka. To take the edge off of the conversation, Boon's father took us to a delicious dinner of Hokkien Chinese food: fried prawns, fresh fruit, black mushrooms, greens, and fried noodles.

After a few days later, we booked passage to the east coast of the Malay peninsula, to visit our old stomping grounds. The bus was supposed to be air conditioned, with reserved seats and toilets on board. When we boarded, there were none of those conveniences, and the sliding glass windows only opened a bare six inches. Sean slept all over me during the hot trip, but we made it in one piece, sweating profusely, to Kota Bharu, in Kelantan state. There we found the Temenggong Hotel, and ate dinner at a Thai restaurant. The Thailand that Nate had lived and worked in as a Peace Corps Volunteer was only a couple of hours north across the border. We had visited once when we lived there in the 1970s, walking over the bridge on the Kelantan River, then taking a trishaw from Malaysia to the border of Thailand, and a train to his former home in the town of Yala.

I could see that the crafts available in Kota Bharu were essentially the same—lovely paper kites and Kelantan filigreed silver jewelry. The batiks had a completely new contemporary look, and some were painted onto rayon with a resist, instead of the traditional cotton sarong. While walking around, we discovered we could get refreshing and sweet banana, papaya, guava, mango, and pineapple squeezed juice. A step up from the old fresh orange drink.

This time we got a Mercedes Benz taxi to Kuala Terengganu, another place that Nate had worked with Volunteers as Peace Corps Regional Representative. This ride was excellent, over good roads, and beautiful scenery along the distant coast. We passed plantations of oil palms, the Terengganu River, and, at last, the South China Sea. We found the old Government Rest House, now the elegant Pantai Hotel, where we enjoyed the view over the water, once again, and experienced the unique opportunity of a partial eclipse of the moon, with its lovely rust-red shadow. The next day was Friday, the Muslim holy day, so all of the old batik shops I used to frequent were closed. Instead we took another Mercedes taxi to Kuantan, Pahang—Nate's and my first home.

The scenes along the way reminded us of the past, uncrowded with vast open spaces between roomy wooden houses on stilts, shaded by palms and cooled by the sea breezes. The only difference was the new-to-us oil refineries, electrical plants and gas refineries. Wealth had come to the east coast of the old Malaya. Upon arriving at the outskirts of Kuantan, we immediately checked out the beach of Telok Chempedak. It was almost unimaginable that this quiet area now had two huge hotel resorts.

The old Rest House where Windi had eaten sand looked the same. I could hardly believe that I was back and looking at my now ten- and fifteen-year-old kids enjoying the view. We sat on the giant rocks at the end of the beach and talked about our life there in the seventies, and about what it was like to give birth to Windi in Malaysia. Then we rented a car (at the new Hyatt Hotel) and drove around looking for our old home. After making two mistakes in identifying the house, and photographing them as well, we found the real one, on Jalan Dato Mahmud. It had changed dramatically, but improved too, with an extended carport, decorative ironwork, and fancy landscaping. Someone had lovingly maintained it. Driving through the rest of the town we took in Nate's old office in the Kuantan Hotel. Cold Storage was still there, but Hock Lee's was gone. The open air market was yet there, but so was the still old decrepit expatriate Kuantan Club that we had refused to join.

The next day we tried to find a quiet beach for Sean, without tourists. We found Gebeng again, where we had previously discovered so many untethered glass balls floating down from Japan. It was the same, but sadly, no glass balls decorated the beach, only ordinary flotsam and jetsam, plus a few shells, like cuttlefish, clams, and broken nautilus. We used to sun and fish here along the white beach, bordered by azure blue water. It was good to be back and the kids loved it.

Suddenly, breaking the serenity of our day, a group of Malay teenagers invaded our space with their cassette decks, mod jeans and carefree ways. But they were friendly and invited the kids to play ball with them, which they did eventually. It was amazing to see such free, sophisticated Malay teenagers. The guys took off their jeans to bright swim shorts, matching their punk hairdos, as they kind of slunk around. But the girls went into the bushes to change, swimming in shorts and tee shirts. This never would have happened in the 1970s. I wondered if they were aping western ways, or just had a lot of privilege, time, and freedom that teenagers didn't enjoy the last time we were here.

Before leaving Kuantan, we visited the new Craft Center. There I stopped at a batik shop and discovered the work of Saidy Malek, the first man to have taught me how to make batik. Saidy didn't

The author with son, Sean, resting on a beach in Kuantan, Pahang, Malaysia, talking about his parents' life there in the 1970s. 1986.

Daughter, Windi, sitting on a rock with father, Nate, on a beach in Kuantan, 1986.

Saidy Malek, my Malay teacher of batik when we lived in Kuantan, Pahang, Malaysia, in his studio with his batik paintings, 1986.

recognize me at first, until I told him my name. When I asked about his brother, Ramli, from whom I had bought batik cloth for export to the States, also a professor at the University of Malaysia, Saidy told me that Ramli had drowned three years ago in a fishing accident. I was sad to learn about Ramli, but I was glad Saidy and I had reconnected.

On our last day, we enjoyed a great Chinese meal downtown in one of the cafes: duck with vegetables, *dim sum*, and two orders of sweet and sour prawns. Having returned our rental car, a Mercedes Benz taxi was waiting to take us over the mountains to Kuala Lumpur and the west coast. There we had been informed by Noordin and Zakinah, our Malay friends and former neighbors, that they had paid for a room for us at a hotel. They would pick us up, so we had lunch at Wendy's, which both kids loved, and tried to find the Peace Corps Office (gone) and our old home in KL, which we finally discovered on Chempedak Road. Then we visited my old stomping grounds on Batu Road: the Odeon Theater was there, as was Peiping Lace and Globe Silk, but Robinson's Department Store had disappeared.

Our former neighbors and Malaysian friends, Noordin and Zakinah,
with their children, whom we visited in Kuala Lumpur, Malaysia, 1986.

When Noordin arrived to pick us up in his Toyota van, with a skylight, stereo sound and reclining seats, we were taken aback by all this luxury. It was great to see him again, and to see Zakinah at their home, more beautiful than I remembered her, wearing a shimmering silk crepe caftan. It was fun to meet their four children, including Nazhan, who was Windi's age. They were a Malay family who had done well.

During dinner we asked our hosts how Malaysia had changed since we lived here, especially the ethnic rivalries. Noordin said that outwardly things were better, but inwardly, worse. Malays had often misused the privileges and power granted them by the government. He wondered out loud how long the other groups would tolerate this. Even Malays were divided among themselves, as moderates and ultras. The government wouldn't give in on this issue of privilege without a change in the constitution.

As to the renewal of their Islamic vows, they were positive about this change in direction. Noordin no longer smoked or drank. Zakinah wanted to cover her head, but Noordin said he wasn't ready. She also wanted to make the Haj to Mecca, but he said he was still not ready to do that either.

After we thanked them for everything and said goodnight, I wondered to myself, why I was so obsessed with returning to places of fond memories. Did it complete a circle somehow for me, or did it confirm that you couldn't really go back, that what was past was past? I guessed the answer was both yes and no.

INDONESIA

We were excited to take off again and explore another country together. The Jakarta airport was new, open and hassle free, after an easy flight from KL. Following our arrival, we soon flew to Jogjakarta, also on the island of Java. This lovely and quiet town had long been a cultural center for Indonesia. It represented the old way of doing things. I was impressed by the relative silence of the streets, and the gentleness of the people.

Our Agung Guest House was utterly charming, in a large compound encircling a beautiful garden, with covered verandas

A Javanese female dancer performing with a gamelan orchestra in Jogjakarta, Indonesia, 1986.

A Javanese gamelan orchestra accompanying a wayang kulit puppet show behind the lighted white screen, with the public sitting on the other side. Note the rows of leather puppets to be used, in various scenes, in Jogjakarta, Indonesia, 1986.

and bamboo chairs and tables enveloped in Indonesian batiks. Influenced by ancient Indian textiles, the Indonesia batiks were among the most beautiful handcrafted batiks in the world. Soon, we were out to see what the town had to offer. A *becak* driver appeared out of nowhere, to drive us slowly to a presentation of the Ramayana Ballet. When we arrived there was no one there, so we had our choice of plush seats, first row, center.

The Ramayana itself was the traditional story of an Indian Princess, stolen by the King of Lanka in hopes that she would wed him, but the white monkey, Hanuman, returned her to her Indian lover, Rama. We were impressed by the *gamelan* orchestra, and the talented players who smoked and drank behind the scenes as they played, and sometimes abruptly changed instruments. They appeared to be old men who knew their craft well, apparently putting on this performance every evening, which perhaps accounted for the scanty audience. We all loved the dancers elegant and deliberate movements, as they presented the story, symbolically.

A Javanese woman in Jogjakarta, Indonesia, using a tjanting tool to draw designs on cloth with molten wax as a resist for later dying, 1986.

The next day we had a light lunch at the hotel—a delicious *gado gado* salad covered in peanut sauce, which included cabbage, boiled eggs, cucumbers, tomatoes, sprouts, cooked beans, carrots, and finally, fried tofu. It was delicious with iced tea that tasted like the fragrance of chrysanthemums. We were headed to a *wayang kulit* show, a well-loved shadow play. Animistic by origin, the shadow plays were a way of asking advice from the ancestors, and magically used to ward off evil or natural disasters. With the advance of Hindu Empires, the *wayang kulit* was a favorite way of telling the Ramayana story. Good always triumphed over evil. Meanwhile, in actual time, the man who manipulated the thin leather puppets behind a lighted white sheet used as the screen, also narrated, sang and spoke their parts while directing the gamelan orchestra, too.

We dragged the kids to watch the batik process, which set the highest standard of textile art in Indonesia. Even though they initially resisted, I thought it was important for them to see. This was women's work, primarily. First a design was hand-drawn on paper, then placed on a glass lit from behind, and traced in pencil onto cotton cloth. Next, the lines were waxed in detail by the artists

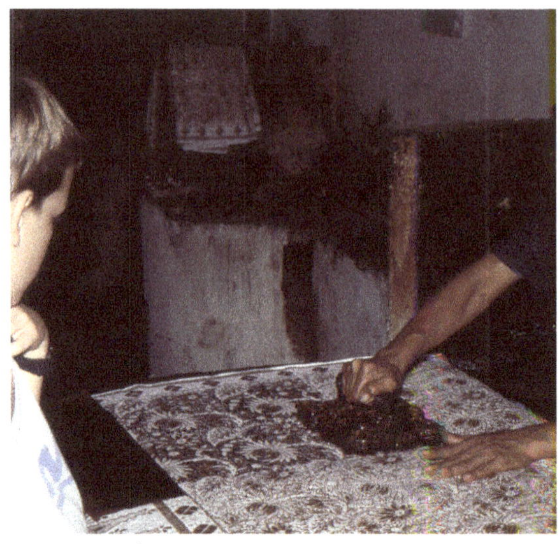

*Sean watching a Javanese man use a tjap,
dipped in molten wax, to print a resist design
onto cloth which will later be dyed, during our
visit to Jogjakarta, Indonesia, 1986.*

with *tjantings*, a tool which was constantly dipped into molten wax. The waxing was done at least several times, on both the front and back of the cloth. This insured the quality and demonstrated the same exact design on both sides. In a less complicated Indonesian batik, a tjap was used, basically a copper stamp in which the design was embedded, exactly how contemporary Malaysian batik was done. The last effort was in the dyeing. After dyeing light colors, other darker colors could be added, while wax was taken off or added, as needed. This was a very complex technique for both our kids, but, surprisingly, they got quite engaged with the process. I bought a couple of traditional batik sarongs with the *kris* design in indigo and brown. I was the only one who liked it.

The following day was an active one. We set out for Borobudur, across the Dieng plateau and around three volcanoes. The goal was to visit a large stone Buddhist monument. Built in the eighth or ninth century AD by a dynastic ruler, its purpose was to illustrate the life of Buddha, his path to enlightenment, and the cosmos itself. Although it was said to be one hundred feet high originally, it was now about ninety feet high. A circular monument took us through nine levels, from desire to formlessness. We all climbed each circle to the top. I found it to be very beautiful and peaceful, with stunning vistas at every level.

The concepts, the details, and the execution of Borobudur marked it as exceptional. Indonesia had been connected to Islam for a very long time, but it manifested the religion in a very laid back Javanese way. To me that indicated a wonderful ability the Javanese had of integrating foreign influences. Here the women wore the *sarong kebaya*, a lacy type of blouse punctuated with a wrapped and pleated batik cloth in front. No women I saw had their head covered. We were lucky to see some classical dancing, different from the Ramayana ballet. The women wore a cummerbund around their waist and their hair in a bun, while the men, bare-chested, had inserted a kris into the top of their sarong. They danced in a sophisticated and stately manner.

We went everywhere in the becak which emphasized for us the slow moving pace of life here. Very few cars were visible. The houses were very creatively arranged. And the food was exceptional. At lunch, before heading up to the temple complex at Prambanan, we splurged at the fancy Garuda Hotel. Our food choices were an eclectic mix of western and Asian food: lamb chops for Sean;

A beautiful frieze along the walls of the Buddhist monument, Borobudur, in Java, Indonesia, 1986.

Chicken Bali for Nate, sirloin strips in hot lava rocks for Windi, and sweet and sour pork for me.

The ancient site of Prambahan had been a Hindu Temple compound, built during an Indian empire in the ninth century AD. The three temples were devoted to different gods: one devoted to Siva, the destroyer, one to Brahma, the preserver, and one to Vishnu, the creator. Interestingly, opposite each one were their respective animal temples: Siva became the Bull, Vishnu the Garuda Bird, and Brahma, the swan. There were also sculptures at each cardinal point in the complex. Again I was struck by how Buddhism, Hinduism, and Islam had developed in Indonesia, how they were somehow intertwined in lasting ways, throughout Indonesian culture.

There was an interesting local myth surrounding the Kali statue and his consort. A young maiden was sought after by the king, to be his wife. She didn't want to marry him but she was afraid of the king, because he had already killed her father. She agreed to marry him if he could produce one thousand temples in one night. He concurred, since he had magical powers. But she tricked him by getting the village women to arise early to pretend the dawn had arrived, and before the thousand temples could be finished. When the cock crowed early, the temple building stopped. The King was so annoyed that he turned the maiden into stone.

It was our last night in Jogjakarta and I traded a Grover Washington cassette with the hotel owner for one of gamelan music. Our final dinner was *rijsttafel,* meaning "rice table," a Dutch name for sampling many Indonesian dishes at one dinner—mostly for tourists. The Dutch had occupied Indonesia from 1602 to 1945, a span of about three hundred fifty years.

The next morning we packed our bags while Windi talked with a young Javanese man who said he was a student of languages. He had very soft manners and I liked him. As a result, I left a used pair of LL Bean pants for him so that I could fit my batiks into my backpack. Then off we went to the airport, where our plane was waiting. It left exactly on time for Bali.

My previous trip to Bali was enchanting. I was eager to see

what had changed, if anything. We decided to rent a car this time and soon a Volkswagen Safari Wagon and a map appeared before us. We took off for Ubud, a village known for its arts and culture. Sean was navigating in the back seat as we carefully drove around people walking in the streets. We had reservations at Hotel Puri Saren, or so I thought. This hotel was supposed to be within a palace compound in Ubud. When we finally landed near it, I walked over the high threshold, guarding against evil spirits, to inquire. At first I was told that there were no rooms available. But Windi urged me to tell the gentlemen that our travel agent had sent a cable a month ago. The man said he would check, then we were told we could have two rooms. Good for Windi.

The palace was actually a series of apartments built around a huge courtyard, each one attached to a large graceful pavilion. The architecture was original: beautiful carvings along the pavilion walls and hand-carved Balinese doors painted in gold leaf. Windi could hardly believe her eyes. Even Nate, who had negotiated the price, loved it. We had two giant rooms back to back, with the pavilions on both ends, surrounded by monkeys, birds, and even peacocks

Our exotic temporary home in Bali, at Puri Saren, within the palace grounds in the village of Ubud, Indonesia, 1986.

in the courtyard. In the center of our pavilion a gorgeous hand-carved circular table with six chairs sitting on an oriental rug was waiting for us. We could barely accept the fact that all of this was ours for the duration.

Hunger dragged us away from all this comfort and beauty. At the Lotus Café it was obvious that many Europeans and Americans had visited, even lived, in Bali since last I was here. The menu was a combination of Balinese, health food, and gourmet choices, like brown rice salad with raisins, cashews and pineapple, and chicken avocado salad with homemade mayonnaise. We ate it up, literally and figuratively.

We were told that there was to be a dance performance that evening somewhere nearby, so we walked to the venue. I knew it would be in stark comparison to the Javanese dancing and gamelan music. I was not wrong, as the exciting, visually striking, and brisk music took everyone except me by surprise. The kids really liked it. They were mesmerized.

It was easy to see how people often stayed months or years, working and living in Bali. Comparatively inexpensive, the culture was so authentic, with festivals, cremations, and other events going on almost constantly throughout the island. I was afraid for the future, though, concerned that tourism would eventually beat back the spirit of the traditions here. In nearly every compound there were artists of one kind or another. How long would the next generation remain interested? For now, however, I resolved not to dwell on the future, but to enjoy the fantastic present.

The following morning began with a breakfast good enough for royalty in our own pavilion: crepes filled with bananas, topped with coconut shavings and local brown sugar, plus boiled eggs, toast, cinnamon/pineapple jam, and coffee or tea. After a family conversation, and because Sean wanted to swim, we headed east to find a beach. Luckily we chanced upon a very beautiful "Bali-Hai" stretch of beach, with a small sign that said Balinese Beach Resort. After a quick consensus, we went inside. Not quite finished, but open, we entered into a room to change, and came out to listen to a man gently playing a sort of bamboo gamelan instrument.

Two traditional Balinese female dancers performing in Bali, Indonesia, during our visit there. Note the difference in costumes with the Javanese dancers, 1986.

The resort was in a little fishing village, beside a rice paddy, with the beach extending off to the horizon. While Sean built a dam in the sand, the rest of us walked the beach. We talked briefly with people, Nate and I trying out our Malay, which was very similar to the Bahasa Indonesia language. We checked out a fisherman's catch, and observed old lava flows. This foray was followed by drinks and lunch in one of the pavilions at the resort. The menu was simple but tasty and nourishing: fried chicken, fish, and noodles.

By the time we drove back to Ubud, it was pitch black. No street lights, no houses with electric lights, and almost no vehicles. But, in the end, we did find our way to our palace home. We decided to eat dinner at a place called The Nomad where we consumed, among other things, banana smoothies and guacamole with prawn chips. But everyone there was *orang puteh*, white. They also looked very 'with it' and reserved, almost whispering. This atmosphere did not easily take our family's talkative and sometimes argumentative style of communicating. As a result I kept shushing everyone in our family. Being here with all of these white people seemed to depress

The author with daughter, Windi, and son, Sean, preparing to enter a Balinese temple in our appropriate sarongs and scarves. Our wearing of windbreakers indicates that it was raining, Indonesia, 1986.

Nate. The kids were a little annoying with each other too, perhaps too much togetherness on this trip. Like me, this was not what Nate was hoping for in Bali. We hoped that tourism wasn't changing everything, conveniently forgetting that we were also tourists.

The following day we learned that there was a temple festival in the village of Sayan. It began at five pm, so after showering, we all changed into our new batik sarongs and added temple scarves we had purchased that morning. Both sarongs and scarves were required temple wear. When we had a hard time finding the nearby village, we asked a Balinese along the way. We slowly followed him down the road to the temple, where people were gathering to eat, bringing offerings, preparing the gamelan orchestra, and making decorations. We felt lucky to be the only foreigners present. When we politely asked to enter the temple, we were welcomed since we were appropriately dressed. Inside the offerings were piling up: two kinds of rice cakes, fruit, peanut brittle, nuts and pancakes. When we left, we watched the offerings being blessed from a distance.

To start the next day, we first got rid of all the little chores of traveling: reconfirming our flights, checking cables and telexes, buying more notebooks, postcards, etc. Taking off into the country always seemed to be the panacea to follow more mundane tasks. So, we headed north to a huge volcanic crater. A little sunshine, some blue skies and a mild breeze in our hair tended to brighten up any day. The crater itself was spectacular and huge, perhaps twelve kilometers across. Sean begged to go down and walk on the freshest lava he could find. We drove down as far as we could, then watched his progress, but it seemed he began to find the going a little scary and quiet, as he walked alone. He soon turned back.

As we wound back on another route home, we climbed up to nearly 4,000 feet, and found it quite cold, even though the villagers along the way were very warm and friendly. They smiled and greeted us and we drove slowly by. We were eager to get back to Ubud for the famous *Recak* or Monkey Dance. Upon arrival, for all of us, the dancing was a spectacular disappointment, very commercial, more like a spectacle than a dance. Nothing like I remembered from before, where the dance was very synchronized and built up gradually to a stunning climax. By contrast, this one was almost slovenly, with no real artistry. We were not Indonesians, of course, but this looked inauthentic. The audience was composed of all foreigners, most drinking liquor while they watched. We left quickly as soon as it was over. Fortunately, as we stepped across the Balinese threshold to our rooms in the palace, a gamelan orchestra was rehearsing and young girls were dancing to it in the authentic Balinese style. It was kind of a 'jam' session, really, and much more interesting and enjoyable than the Monkey Dance performance we had just left.

Finally, we had reached our last day in Bali. We learned that there would be a cremation ceremony today, very important in Balinese culture. Arriving at the designated village just in time, we saw the nine-story platform being carried by many men. Inside was the casket of the deceased person. As the men walked they shook the structure to disorient the spirit of the deceased so that he wouldn't find his way back home. Meanwhile, water was constantly being thrown at the bearers to keep them cool. The body was ultimately taken out of the casket and put into a decorated bull sarcophagus, sitting astride a pyre. Several ceremonial ablutions were made before the sarcophagus was set ablaze by a torch connected to a tank of gas. This was definitely a modern version of a cremation ceremony compared to the mid 1960s.

After about forty-five minutes, the bottom of the box was pried loose so that the body could fall into a sort of wire basket, continuing to burn in full view. Children and adults participated and watched. It was not an occasion for grieving but for rejoicing as the body was being returned to the earth and the spirit set free. Afterwards, the bones were stirred into ash and put inside an empty coconut. Then the coconut was wrapped in a batik cloth and carried to the sea where the ashes would be spread. At this special occasion, we were fortunate to have been able to witness such a sacred ritual.

As I contemplated our time in Bali, I had lots of unanswered questions. How did the economy function? Why were there no beggars? How do people support themselves doing so many creative things, primarily for themselves? How do they express their anger,

A traditional cremation ceremony in Bali, Indonesia, which we witnessed while visiting there in 1986. The body was burned in a magnificently decorated palanquin.

in a culture that wants to keep things balanced? What is courtship and marriage like? How long will the youth be able to keep this unique way of life going, given the worldwide western influence?

As we packed and prepared to leave the next morning, we all felt a little sad. Journeying through this fascinating culture had been a special experience for all of us. Windi even said, "You know, I really loved Bali. When we get home, I will take another look at our many Asian things, which I have ignored until now." Good enough for me.

THE PHILIPPINES

While Sean was up front talking with the captain on the flight out of Jakarta, Windi was reading a novel, Nate was writing to Gamini Dissanayake in Sri Lanka and I was watching us cross Sabah, North Borneo. Lovely to be flying low and slow over the jungles, river mouths, and tin-roofed houses down below. After waking at four a.m. to prepare for a six a.m. departure, the sun had just started to redden the eastern horizon when we left Bali. Suddenly, it seemed, we had already landed in Kota Kinabalu, the former Jesselton of my Peace Corps days.

During our few hours wait, we called our parents to check in, wrote letters, and exchanged currency, then took off for Manila. We were low enough when we flew over Sabah's striking Mount Kinabalu to see it encircled by mist, with a miniature view of the village of Kundasang below. Flying over the Philippines, we passed near the island of Palawan, but I couldn't see the small island of Culion where I had worked with the children of lepers. We also flew over Oriental Mindoro, but I could barely see the mountains where I had worked with the Mangyans in the summer of 1966.

In Manila, we were staying with an American family we had met in Sri Lanka, primarily because Windi was a friend of their daughter, Cindy. Leroy was a USAID/State Department career employee. His Vietnamese wife, Le, was gracious and hospitable, as they picked us up in their Mercedes Benz and took us to their lovely home in the wealthy Magallanes Village, where many expatriates lived. I was in awe of their lifestyle.

Over dinner, Leroy talked about the Philippines under President Corazon Aquino, the wife of the assassinated former president. He felt rather negative about her leadership. She abolished the Constitution, the Supreme Court, and replaced all the elected officials in the towns and cities with her supporters. According to Leroy, half of her four closest advisors had communist party leanings. Apparently, when the votes were recounted she didn't come up the winner, so that angle was dropped and a revolutionary presidency was established. Leroy didn't think she had the support she needed. She may have been a communist, because she released communists from jail who were there for murder. I didn't know what to say because I hadn't kept up on Filipino politics since leaving the country.

We were eager to get in touch with Father Postma, so that we could arrange for our travel back to visit the Mangyans.* Meanwhile, we were wined and dined by Le and Leroy, enjoying a great scallop dinner at Seafront, the club inside the American Embassy in Manila. The next day, Windi went to the American School with Cindy. Sean stayed home to watch television (which he hadn't seen in years). I shopped around Ermita, landing in Tesoros department store. This was where my mother back in 1966 bought an embroidered dress made of pineapple fiber for me. A beautiful gown, it had only cost her fifty dollars. She thought it a good value for a future wedding dress, even in the sixties. There I bought some silver earrings to share with Wili and my namesake, Susan, when we got to Panatayan. Nate bought a small basketball set for the young ones, toy jeeps, pencils, fancy erasers and decorated notebooks for the kids.

In the meantime, we hired a car to travel to Malolos, my home and teaching assignment for nearly two years. The town looked much the same to me, the big Catholic Church still in its center, the town hall still there, and lastly, Malolos Pilot Elementary school turned up before we landed in my old barrio. Emma, now married with children, greeted us from the front porch of the house I had lived in. It was fun to meet her three boys, although her husband was working elsewhere. I already knew that the rest of the family had moved to Canada. Emma didn't seem very surprised to see us, perhaps I had written her earlier, I couldn't remember. Nevertheless, Emma sent to get my old friend and co-teacher, Ella, and the parents of my godson, Elmer, so we could go for lunch. There wasn't time to invite all of the teachers I might have enjoyed seeing again. I thought we were heading out to the well-known Valenzuela restaurant on the highway, but it appeared to no longer exist. We accidentally changed restaurants without informing Elmer's parents of the change.

Fortunately, we were able to meet my godson's parents separately after lunch. They brought out cakes and Cokes and we gave them a card plus five hundred pesos for Elmer. Ironically, he was arriving the following night, so we missed him completely. Elmer had made his parents proud when he joined the Merchant Marines, where he was doing very well. A real pleasure for our family and their family to connect. Although not wealthy, the father had saved enough money to purchase some land for each of his two sons. Impressive.

The Bayanihan Dance troupe performing the tinikling dance where the dancers jump between bamboo poles clicking together, Manila, the Philippines, 1986.

Before we headed to Mindoro and beyond, I wanted Nate and the kids to see an authentic cultural performance of the Bayanihan Dance Troupe. I had met them a couple of times when I lived there, and just loved these talented and friendly young people. So, we headed to the Manila Hotel and bought tickets. It was a gorgeous and exciting performance of many cultural dances, everyone dressed in traditional costumes, many being the ones the Spaniards had introduced during their colonization. The men wore shirts called *barong tagalog* while the women were dressed in gowns with the big elegant butterfly sleeves that stood above their shoulders. We all loved every minute of this wonderful presentation.

After our visit to the Mangyans, we were off to China. Our experience was dimmed a bit at the airport, especially for me. We had never been searched so personally before. An officer pulled an individual Tampax out of my bag, and held it up by the string as if it were a fuse, and asked what it was. I was considerably put off, being embarrassed publicly, in front of everyone in line. That beginning to our trip to China, along with my relative lack of interest in the next country, made for a bad start. But Nate had always wanted to see China, and the kids were gung ho, so off to Beijing we went.

I described our visit to the Mangyans, as part of my experience with them when I was a Peace Corps Volunteer, in the section entitled "The Mangyans," in the chapter on The Philippines.

CHINA

During a fairly unmemorable flight to Beijing, with seats covered in pale blue cloth, the flight attendants, wearing loose turquoise pant suits, spoke English reasonably well. Lunch looked unappetizing, so I only ate the roll and a dry piece of cake. The airport in Beijing was austere, but a friendly guide met us in an air-conditioned bus, so it wasn't all bad. The hotel, outside of the city was new and nice, better than any we had stayed in before. Dinner at seven-thirty consisted of four cold plates of salami, pickled cucumbers, bean sprouts and chicken. The four hot dishes consisted of pork spareribs, pork and bean sprouts, green veggies in oyster sauce, eggs and tomatoes, soup and fish. It wasn't what I was expecting in China, though I realized Chinese restaurants at home were very different. It was a pretty bland meal, but nothing to complain about in quantity and quality. In addition, the kids enjoyed a snack bar offering Sprite, Coca Cola, pinwheel cookies, almond cookies, Chinese chocolates and cake. And our room was air conditioned. What more could we ask for? My spirits were rising to meet the challenge of China.

My first impressions of the city were that it was smoggy, colorless, drab and dusty with lots of construction. Not much greenery, but enormously wide streets, little traffic, and lots of cyclists. I learned that the population of Beijing was nine million, and that three million rode bicycles. The citizens walked steadily and slowly, perhaps purposefully. Serious, sullen, happy: I wasn't sure. That first day we did the usual touristy things, among them, standing in a half-mile line to see the somewhat waxy-looking face of Mao Tse Tung's body. Everyone, including us, appeared quiet and respectful. His mausoleum was in Tienanmen Square, considered the largest in the world, where half a million people could stand together, I was told.

We were only allowed to travel in and around China with a guide. We were lucky in that we were just one family, not a large American group. Our guide was called Mr. Yu, but we could call him 'Roger'. A young man, he said that he expressed a choice among limited selections for a job and was assigned this one. Nearly everyone earned close to the same thing from the government: doctors to ditch diggers, he said. Incentives were offered by bonuses for good work. He also got more bonuses for leading more tours. He further told us that China had mandatory abortions of fines after the birth of one child. I didn't realize this. He also told us that there was some crime, but not much.

We all enjoyed a thrilling evening at the Chinese Ballet, which told the story of a Han Dynasty Princess who married a Tibetan King to bring the two nationalities together. Beautiful dancing, fabulous costumes, a moving and touching performance. Afterwards we returned to the hotel for dinner, which consisted first of donuts and peanuts, and ended in ice cream this time. I was reminded that the Chinese had invented ice cream.

I was eager to see what else China offered. The guidebook said that the Chinese were "graceful, dignified, unhurried, and satisfied, if not overindulged…" I decided that Beijing did possess a certain stateliness, uncrowded and clean, no littering or spitting allowed. Socialism seemed to be a great equalizer, but I'd never been anywhere that everyone dressed nearly the same, regardless of their education or profession. Did that eliminate greed? What happened when more private enterprise developed? Would there be more satisfaction or more discontent? What if nine million people drove cars instead of bicycles?

Sean couldn't wait to see the Great Wall of China, and the rest of us were pretty curious too. We climbed a structurally sound section of the wall, but we could see many places where it was disintegrating. After all, the wall was begun more than 2,000 years ago and finished in 200 BC, mostly with rocks and packed earth to keep the Mongol invaders out. It was the only man-made object visible from space. That alone was amazing. I imagined that I could see Mongolia over the distant mountains. It was good to be in the sunny, dry clear air with the wind blowing across one of the wonders of the world.

That night we had our last meal in Beijing, and it was a fantastic feast. The various courses included: Century eggs, cold meats, bean curd noodles, mushrooms, and mandarin oranges first. Then we were served cooked egg whites with scallops, giant sweet and sour prawns, and finally, Beijing Duck. But that wasn't all, the meal continued with lovely green beans, large mushrooms, cauliflower with ham, barbecued eel, and duck soup. Along with as much to drink as we wanted, plus Chinese red wine, there were desserts of lychees, pears, and mandarin oranges on ice. We loved it, suddenly realizing that was probably the best meal we would have in China.

On our way to the airport, Mr. Yu expressed his genuine wish for Americans and Chinese to get together more often. I was moved

Our family on the Great Wall of China, 1986, the only man-made object in the world that can be seen from space.

by this, as I think we all were and we expressed the same sentiment to him. Then Sean asked if China was still a communist country. It was an awkward and funny moment, but we were all interested in the answer. Mr. Yu said communism was a system whereby workers work for the good of their country. Capitalism, he said, was where people work for an individual, a private company or themselves. We agreed that communism more directly benefited the government, and vice versa; whereas, hopefully, in capitalism the government was benefited indirectly. It was a good and memorable moment. I felt very warmly towards Mr. Yu when we shook hands to say goodbye. Sean gave him the envelope of money we had collected along with a note we all signed.

En route to Xi'an, we were given a box lunch on the plane, which consisted of pureed apricots and a box of Danish cookies, half a ham sandwich, a box of candy, and a China Airlines key chain. Our new guide, Mr. Li, seemed very precise and polite and looking like he might have graduated from Harvard—long hair, horn rimmed glasses, blazer, and leather boots. As he didn't seem very forthcoming with information, Nate determined later that he had just graduated from the university and only worked part time as a guide, which he didn't really like. He majored in American literature, and was waiting to be a translator. Meanwhile, he studied English and earned about ten US dollars a month to guide. He thought his supervisor earned maybe eighty *yuan* or about thirty US dollars a month. He told Nate that the top government officers would have houses of their own. Others below them would have a little larger and a little more comfortable apartments than those at his level.

Our mission today was to see the recently excavated terracotta warrior statues discovered in 1974 by peasants digging a well. The statues represented an army of a Qin emperor, which supposedly covered some twenty-five square kilometers. Perhaps 8,000 statues would ultimately be found. The amazing thing was the depiction of different, individual faces and hair-dos. I was absolutely riveted to the scene below me. The question was, were these warriors buried with the emperor (killed), or buried after a natural death? I took out my camera to take a photo, which I knew was against the rules, and sure enough, a Chinese official accosted me, by shouting in words I didn't understand. Luckily, he didn't take my camera.

We were able to see some semi-underground homes from a neolithic site. These homes gradually developed into above-ground houses. Mr. Li also showed us a boundary ditch, dividing clans, with a dug moat to keep out wild animals and drain off water. I was amused because Nate's ancient ancestors had also put up a boundary ditch between warring Somerset and Dorset tribes in England, sometime in the twelfth century, thus the name, 'Bowditch'.

Walking around Xi'an, we saw young children, brightly dressed, coming down the street and singing while holding onto a rope to keep them together. They must have been in some kind of daycare so their parents could work. That evening, as the sky mellowed into dusk we took another walk after dinner. We had a good time trying to talk with shopkeepers who were very friendly. Sean and Windi attracted quite a crowd while they bargained for brush paintings at two for six yuan. Windi chose a horse, and Sean, a warrior. Inside one store we got into a lengthy discussion with a young woman who was studying English at night school and spoke very well. She said she had to learn one hundred new words a week. We helped her out with "outstanding," "sightseeing," and "scholarship." What a great candidate to study abroad, I thought, but I doubted she would get the chance.

The next day, Mr. Li gave us a choice as to what to see. Nate wanted to see the mosque, which appealed less to the rest of us. But it was lovely. I am sure I expected something modern and middle-eastern looking, but it was very Chinese in style. Interestingly, the mosque was also on a side street or alley, and our first opportunity to wander behind the living quarters to observe people at their daily tasks. There were also a lot of little doorway-shops, some selling these wonderful embroidered silk caps for children, with fantastic animal faces atop the cap.

The tree-lined main street was quaint and fun too. A wonderful old man approached Sean and laughed and talked to him in some Chinese language. Apparently he had witnessed Sean arguing with his father and wanted to comment on it. Another bright-looking young man stopped and asked us to explain a word from the newspaper: "paralyzed," as it applied to a strike in Bangladesh. Then he quoted something from an IBM computer manual that he didn't understand: "When the continuous paper is present, the card sheet is unusable." We all had a good laugh over that, and suggested he write IBM for more information, as we had no idea what it meant.

We continued walking around the streets of Xi'an, looking at fried buns filled with green vegetables, pao being kept warm in huge baskets, very thick and sticky wheat noodles being made—as well as a man repairing men's black shoes and slippers. Sean was looking for a pair, but we failed to find any his size. So we packed him off with Mr. Li, and after some time Sean returned with a pair about an inch too long, and an inch too wide, but a big smile on his face.

Xi'an, famous for being the start of the "Silk Road," an ancient trading route from China to Europe and back, still appeared to be quite a shopper's marketplace, compared to Beijing. Whether those two things connected, I didn't know.

Sean buying something from market sellers in Xi'an, China, 1986.

A Chinese man and woman making shoes on the street in Xi'an, China, 1986.

Our time in Xi'an was almost over. After a lunch of sole, chips and green beans, we took off for the airport. Upon our departure, we gave Mr. Li a note with some money in an envelope. He refused it, saying it was prohibited. I admired his honesty and wondered why Mr. Yu had accepted it. We learned that he liked to read contemporary love stories by Joyce Carol Oates, so we said we would send him some of her books.

Our flight to Guilin was smooth and comfortable, despite the fact that it was only a propeller plane and we sat next to the bathroom in the back. Guilin appeared warm, and the shrubs, grass and flowers represented the subtropics now. Our new guide, Mr. Shen, had been waiting for us since nine a.m., and we arrived at five. But he was young and kind, taking us first to our hotel to settle in before anything else. The town itself seemed to be even more bustling than Xi'an, with a population of 300,000. Although originating 2,000 years ago, it reminded us of Southeast Asia: open-air stalls, open storefronts, and people bathing in the river.

The next morning, after a hot, somewhat sleepless night, we awoke to a rainy day. This was the day for our six-hour cruise down the Li River. Fortunately, the rain began to stop and we spent three hours observing spectacular limestone formations, each view more fantastic than the last. Formed by movements in the earth's crust thousands of years ago, their pinnacles were once under the sea. This was about the most stunning scenery we had yet experienced in China.

Halfway through the cruise, we stopped at a little riverside village. The small winding streets were lined with shops, mostly for tourists, but I discovered some antiques scattered here and there. Mr. Shen was always having his photo taken by other guides, with his glasses on and off, or with his sunglasses on instead. I do remember that he was very good looking. After the tour we retired to our hotel, which was fairly new but not in prime condition. We were used to traveling in less than first class conditions but I wondered about the upper-crust people from Boston and New York. Despite the carpeting, TV, telephone and errant air conditioner, there was a close view of a construction site, the colors of the room were bright and clashing, with scruffy chenille bedspreads. Not everyone's cup of tea.

I noted that the food got boring over time, even though the dishes were well prepared and numerous, they tended to be bland and the format was almost always the same. I longed for some Thai food, even Mexican, to break the monotony. But, I realized that this country didn't encourage foreign cuisine or commodities, and we actually had nothing to complain about. The food had been nourishing, if not exciting. This was China at the time.

Our evening flight to Guangzhou had been delayed until nearly ten p.m. As Mr. Shen said, CAAC stands for 'China Airlines Always Cancelled." By the time we arrived in the city, formerly called Canton, it was nearly midnight. But the hotel was huge and extremely luxurious by any standard. Our new guide, Miss Ling, said it was a joint venture with the Peninsular Hotel Group in Hong Kong. Aha, private enterprise at work.

After waking up famished the next morning, we took advantage of all the European/American food the hotel offered for breakfast: croissants, Danish pastries, bacon, sausage, fresh orange juice, yoghurt, fresh fruit salad, crepes and poached eggs. This was a lovely breakfast, complete with very hot cups of coffee. Shortly thereafter, Miss Ling introduced us to the goat statues, a monument to the origins of Guangzhou. Five celestial beings came down from the heavens, riding five goats with sheafs of rice in their mouths. They settled, the people began growing rice, and thus the city grew.

We spent the afternoon near the Swan Hotel another great hotel right on the Pearl River. Windi chose to buy a book and sit in the lobby and read while Nate, Sean, and I went across to Shamian Island, an old diplomatic and European-style enclave. There we found the free market in the little alleys. We were seeking out antiques but found even more interesting items. There were the most incredible food choices, as well as herbal medicines, grains, lentils, dried seeds, and weeds we'd never seen before. In addition, we came upon leopard skins, tiger skins, python skins, dried snakes all curled up and piled in burlap bags, furry antlers, and stacks of dried, spraddle-legged frogs. There were also live animals, including turtles, monkeys, and cats piled in cages, alive but smothering in the heat, live eels three feet long slithering all over each other, and catfish crawling around in the bottom of pans. There were also dead ducks in a row, pigs hooves lined up on a counter, and tongues hanging from the hooks. To us, it was amazing as we had never seen anything like this.

Ironically, we followed all we witnessed in that market with genteel iced tea and mango custard in our hotel café. Then Miss Ling took us to a Trade Center in which the semi-annual Guangzhou trade fairs were held. In it we had our last meal in China—suffice it to say it was excellent. We talked with her about women in China. She said that they received the same pay for the same work as men, but marked preference was shown for men in responsible positions, regardless if there was a more qualified woman. In fact, employers often asked for a man since there was no law against it. For university admittance, women were required to have a score of ninety, men of eighty. We commiserated, citing women's problems in the United States.

Now all we had left, was taking the train across the border into Hong Kong. Our China odyssey, and our Asian adventures, were nearly over. It had been a great experience, enjoying something special and unique about each country we had visited. The length of the trip was about right. It was time for a change, to return to the United States and begin our new American adventure.

First, we had to go through the unusually difficult authorities at Kai Tak Airport in Hong Kong. We thought we could still hand carry our backpacks, but for the first time the airlines wouldn't allow it, so we checked our bags and carried a couple of packages. But when we got to customs, they would not allow one package because it was too high, and another because it was too long. So we had to return to the United Airlines counter to get "special permission." Once again, Nate was really fried, the way he always felt about this airport. To top it off, he discovered that the x-ray machines here damaged film, and he didn't know that when he took all of our new undeveloped film to China. It was too staggering to think about, so we decided to defer the possibility of ruined photos to later…

After a few hours we arrived in Tokyo, and found ourselves in the waiting room at Narita Airport. Nate discovered a fourth floor lounge, quiet, and practically empty, with a good view of all the planes. It also had clean bathrooms and comfortable sofas. We regrouped as family, relaxed, beginning to shed our wondrous Asian life and travels. We still had a lot to process, but the next stop was Honolulu, returning full circle to my family.

The author's family reunited once again in Honolulu, Hawaii, on a beach, en route home to Maine from Sri Lanka, 1986. Left to right, back row: the author's brother Carver, the author, daughter Windi, and husband Nate. Left to right, front row: Sister Kathleen's husband Romaine, sister Kathleen, author's son Sean, author's mother and father.

GHANA

The view from our home in Cape Coast, Ghana, to Cape Coast Castle in the distance, and the village of Brofoyedur, below in the foreground. We could see this view every day from our balcony while we lived there, 1990-1994.

CAPE COAST, GHANA

We arrived late at night, flying over dark landscapes to the announcement of bright lights above Accra. In 1990, one still walked off the plane onto the hot tarmac, into the humid air. Our fourteen-year-old son, Sean, and I were taken to a lounge to wait while Nate went through customs and collected our bags. The director of the Central Region Development Commission (CEDECOM), a United Nations' economic development project in the Central Region, waited with us. I asked him what kind of government Ghana had—a democracy, or a monarchy, perhaps. He could barely disguise scoffing at my ignorance, and I was embarrassed that I hadn't done any research at all before coming here. Nate had visited once to look over the job as chief technical advisor. He was excited about the prospects of an opportunity to work and live in Africa. Although always eager for a new adventure, instead I had been focused on finishing my master's degree, getting our house rented, making sure our daughter was okay at Oberlin College, packing up, storing, and otherwise giving away our belongings before departure.

Finally, we organized ourselves to leave the bustling Accra airport—to which international flights came and went only at night—perhaps demonstrating how much Europeans controlled the airport traffic to Ghana. We headed to a small simple hotel in Osu, a section of Accra. Sean had his own room but was scared to sleep by himself, so I took the other single bed. We were all exhausted. However, Nate, with the staff outside on the balcony, watched while liquor libations were poured onto the floor, respecting the ancestors, and bringing good luck to the project.

The next day Nate's new driver, Dramani, came to pick us up in the air conditioned project car for the two-plus hour drive to Cape Coast. He played Bob Marley songs on the tape, while Nate slept in the front seat, and Sean and I froze in the back. I had been told we would stay in a guest house and I imagined something simple, made of wood, maybe on stilts. Ghana was not a wealthy country and we were headed for the now much less glamorous, and much poorer former capital of the British Gold Coast. Upon arriving, I could barely believe that we were to stay temporarily in a lovely home with European furniture, three air conditioned bedrooms, a big living room with attached kitchen, and a huge garden. The furnishings weren't to my taste, but I appreciated sleeping cool at night. Before long we accidentally corrupted our computer on a different electrical platform. That took some time to get corrected. Still, we enjoyed our Panasonic radio with batteries, and the one cassette we happened to have carried with us, which we played almost continuously: "Galway's Irish Flute Concertos."

Within a couple of days, Sean got very ill. Nate called the Central Regional Rep's office to get a recommendation for a doctor. We took Sean there, along with extra needles, in case he needed a shot. We were all worried about AIDS in those days. The doctor said Sean had pneumonia and would get well faster with a shot. Sean adamantly refused, so he took pills and slept around the clock for a week.

Meanwhile, school had been delayed, not unusual, we were to learn. We had already enrolled him in St. Augustine's, a Ghanaian public boy's school, dating back to the British colonial period. He wanted to see it before it started so we all went over. Everything was closed and the lawn was high with weeds, the buildings looked ill-kept, and we could see through the glassless windows the tumble of chairs and tables. Sean was shocked and said he wouldn't go there. We were a little shocked too, but urged him to just try it for a couple of weeks, then we could make a different decision, if necessary. The only alternative would be for Sean and me to live in Accra so that he could attend Lincoln School, an expatriate school which only went up to ninth grade. Not a perfect solution, so we hoped for the best.

In the meantime, our house was being readied to move into. It had been empty for fourteen years, owned by a banker in Accra. I was eager to see it. But first, we had to drive through the very poor village of Brofoyedur to get there. We had to drive slowly because the potholes were so big. Of course that made us very visible and soon people were shouting *"Obroni, obroni,"* meaning "white man." Our new home turned out to top one of those bumpy hills that hovered around the Ghanaian coast and, in this instance, overlooked Broyfoyedur. That village, with its chalky white concrete buildings couldn't begin to house the people that billowed out of them, and meant that just off the street was often the only place to eat, to trade, to urinate, even to sleep. For the entire time we lived there, we drove through it daily. I was ashamed to be in a car going through a neighborhood in which people seemed to have almost nothing, certainly not a car. To try to counter this, we made a habit of stopping to buy something small in one of the little kiosks along the way. We began to say hello to the friendly faces we recognized next to the road.

Sean walking with Dramani, our friend and Nate's project driver, to the home we would live in for four years, Brofoyedur village, Cape Coast, Ghana, 1990. From the balcony, Cape Coast Castle was easily visible.

As we drove up the steep driveway to the house which was to be our home for the next four years, I thrilled when we stopped at the top. The house itself, a rather large concrete rectangle, shot straight up one side and down the other. Despite a yard of dirt, the view from the second floor balcony was amazing. Here, for the first time, we could see Cape Coast Castle in the near distance to our right, about a half mile away as the crow flies. Our house overlooked the point where the castle, a large triangular structure, perched precariously on a point jutting into the Atlantic Ocean. We could also see much of the rest of Cape Coast, including other hills with houses on the tops, and through fairly dense jungle to our left, down to a beach fringed with palms.

I had yet to visit Cape Coast Castle, but Nate had told me a little bit about it. Built in the sixteenth century as a legitimate trading port between the Fantis and the Europeans, it disintegrated into a pickup stop for The Atlantic Slave Trade. I learned that this castle was the site of dark negotiations, fetid underground floors, and human holding tanks. The enslaved persons imprisoned here in the past were captured in the north of present-day Ghana by the Asante people. Our view was a daily reminder of that shameful past in which our country both participated and profited. That was what got my attention, so I was somewhat keen, but also conflicted to visit it soon.

Meanwhile, we had a look at where we would live. Empty, it had very little charm, except for the second floor balcony which extended across the width of the house and about twenty feet forward. Behind that, inside, stretched a large hall, off of which were four plain bedrooms and two bathrooms. The kitchen downstairs was enormous, but not very convenient. The sink and counters were at a window, but the fridge and stove were on the opposite wall, about twenty feet away.

Fortunately, the next day, the contractor, Papadu, came by and offered to take me to Accra to order furniture and pick out fabrics. I was delighted to be invited as I took pleasure in decorating our overseas homes with local fabrics. In Accra we ordered several pieces of simple rattan furniture for all the rooms. For the living room sofa cushions, I picked out black and white *adinkra* cloth, used traditionally for mourning. I first asked if this was acceptable culturally, as I wanted to be very careful. The answer was affirmative, although I was cautioned not to buy the beautiful handwoven *kente* cloth for dining tables or beds, which would have been disrespectful.

For the dining room, I chose local batik fabrics. I also selected "African cloth" printed designs for cushions and pillows on the rattan chairs upstairs in the hall. Finally, for our bedroom I discovered a green adinkra cloth with the traditional multicolor threads—yellow, green, red and blue—connecting several pieces together. And on our way back to Cape Coast, in a village called Winneba, I bought some pottery to grace our table. All of this was provided for in the contract Nate had with the United Nations.

I realized how lucky I was to be able to do this. I felt some guilt too, because our neighbors in Brofoyedur were so poor. Eventually, Nate, in particular, would find a way to help several of the local kids. I, personally, expected to treat everyone equally, not give out money. But I was wrong, in the sense that we were not all equal financially. So, I watched as Nate helped Kwasi Patrick get a bicycle so he could sell ice cream. In return Kwasi had to help another bright boy, Kojo, learn to read. Although Kojo wasn't very cooperative, his confidence level rose. Finally, Nate helped a young man named Kakra to learn how to repair cars.

I, on the other hand, in the spirit of equality, decided to talk with a group of young school girls who greeted me each day in Brofoyedur. They always said "hello obroni." I asked their names and told them mine. They were very serious-looking when I asked them to call me "Susie," and I would try to remember their names when I said hello. But when I said goodbye, they said: "Goodbye, Obroni." Some things were hard to change.

In the meantime, I couldn't wait for our home to come together so that I could spend the rest of my time meeting people and exploring the multi-faceted cultures that were Ghana.

THE UN-HAPPENING DINNER PARTY

The stage was set for guests, an inviting living room of cane and bamboo furniture, the coffee table displaying a few discreet books to help our visitors experience America—mostly from National Geographic. While the batik curtains on the louvered windows disguised the iron bars masked as ivy vines, the concrete floor came alive with rustic pots in small groupings. In the dining room the long table with a glass top was already cracked, a mistake to begin with. But the luscious blue and lavender colors of the tie-dye tablecloth, in concert with the richly glazed plates from the potters at Winneba, and cheap cutlery from the Cape Coast market, said, "Yes, we were ready to entertain."

This was our first dinner party in Ghana. We had just moved into our big old house on a hill above the ocean. It had been empty for many years but the owner had put a fresh coat of paint on it with the prospect of a new long term renter. We turned out to be the new renters.

We had prepared for this day for a couple of weeks, invited Nate's colleagues, our language teacher, and the contractor who had made our house habitable. We knew that it was important to remind everyone of the date a couple of days in advance, and we had dutifully done so. Everyone seemed to be both surprised and delighted that they had been invited to an obroni's house. And we were excited that this would be an opportunity to get to know some of the people who had made our stay here so far, most interesting and pleasant. It was going to be a win-win situation for everyone.

The kitchen was ready with a big apple pie I had made on a cookie sheet at great expense because apples had to be imported from China, but what could be a more American offering than that? Fortunately Angie, who worked for us during the day, and could read a cookbook very well, had baked my favorite crescent rolls ahead. We had sautéed some prawns, and made a salad, whose leaves had been sterilized through the mixing of a few tablespoons of bleach with filtered drinking water. The cold dishes were in the refrigerator and the hot ones were warming in the oven. We were set to go, we just needed our guests.

Dinner was to have been about 6:00, early since we knew that Ghanaians never seem to arrive anywhere on time, at least not by our notion of time. By 9:30 we were very concerned: had there been an accident? A family emergency? A misunderstanding? And then our first guests arrived—with their neighbors, who had stopped by their house around dinner time. The contractor and his wife arrived with their kids sometime later, explaining that they had already eaten but they were coming to socialize. And the language instructor, among others, never made it.

We were totally flummoxed by this situation. We had been so careful to invite people well in advance, presumably so they could put the date on their calendars. Then we had been equally vigilant about little reminders in person in case they forgot, which they assured us they had not. What had happened then?

It took us awhile before we understood that evening's mishap. It took us even longer to understand some of the underlying cultural issues that were in operation in general. And some things we never completely understood.

First, it was helpful to know that Ghanaians considered someone who visited them as the greatest honor. They were not in the habit of issuing specific invitations to individuals or couples. The visitor took priority over everything else, even if you had been invited elsewhere for dinner. So, we were lucky that one of our guests brought their guests to our house.

Secondly, there was always intention, and then there was reality. Things happened, things came up. It was a market culture and everything was negotiable. Very little was set in stone. It was possible that the contractor's family got a better invitation. Or had to do something else that took priority. Even if they fully intended to come to our dinner party, there may have been something either more pressing, or more attractive, which diverted their intentions. At least they eventually showed up with their kids.

Finally, Ghana was a poor country economically. People couldn't afford telephones. In some villages, telephones might be available but the villagers would have had to put up or pay for the poles to install the line to their houses. And few could afford cars which meant that public transportation was the only way to go, and public transport by creaky old buses or packed vans was notoriously unreliable. Sometimes it might just not be worth the effort. And because most individuals had no way to let you know that he or she couldn't get here from there, they just didn't show up. That was what happened to the language instructor, we found out later. End of story.

But this wasn't the end of the story for us, as we stayed nearly seven years in Ghana, doing everything we could to understand what motivated people, and what cultural or practical traditions supported their actions. Eventually we made progress, but Ghana, like most cultures, was very complex. It would take a lifetime to figure it out. We tried our best and loved almost every minute of it. Not always fun, but always engaging.

WHAT WE DID IN CAPE COAST, 1990-1993

Nate had always wanted an opportunity to work in Africa, since we had lived only overseas in Southeast and South Asia. I was interested too. When a colleague told Nate that the United Nations Development Program was looking for a technical advisor on a project in Ghana, he jumped right in and got the job. He would be advising on a very interesting project. The Ghanaian government wanted to create tourism, especially for African Americans, around Cape Coast Castle, as well as nearby Elmina Castle and Fort St. Jago. The agency for this project was The Central Region Development Commission (CEDECOM), as I previously mentioned.

Built originally as a legitimate trading lodge, Cape Coast Castle, then enlarged by the Swedes in 1753, it had been designated a World Heritage Site by the United Nations, a major form of recognition. Many believed it to be a most compelling monument for telling the important story of The Atlantic Slave Trade. Conversely, the Ghanaian government wanted other national markers to have equal place, especially within the creation of a new museum in the castle. The project was pulled in several different directions. Compromises had to be made. A couple of years later, the Midwestern University Consortium for International Activities (MUCIA), entered the picture, working on the same project, and Nate went to work for them.

Nate, the team of Ghanaians, along with other nationals, set out to address all of the issues that related to the tourism goal. The conservation of Cape Coast Castle would be followed by the interpretation of the castle within the museum. The development of hotels and restaurants came next, so that tourists would have adequate facilities when they visited. Finally, the creation of a national park, Kakum, up the road a few miles, would provide jobs for Ghanaians. It would also give tourists an opportunity to see the last bit of the Upper Guinean tropical rain forest, which would include a walkway through the treetops. In total the project was very exciting, but it was also very controversial.

As for conserving Cape Coast castle, authenticity became the goal. This meant literally "white washing" its exterior, applying to the castle walls a mixture primarily made up of crushed shells, chalk and water, the original coating on Cape Coast Castle. The conservation activity included the upper rooms which had previously belonged to the governor of the castle, luxurious rooms furnished with European goods. The best views of the sea were to be had from there. The Palaver Hall where the negotiations over slaves happened was also being conserved. Almost all of the small offices, storage areas, the castle's east side where the big cannons were pointed towards the sea, the parade ground, along with the tombstones and graves on the Castle's floor, and a small church were to be conserved. The dungeons appeared to be excluded.

Obviously, the "white washing" had a double meaning, since several white consultants, including Nate, were involved. Some African Americans thought that white men had no place on the project, because they were largely responsible for what had happened there. Many Black Americans, who lived in the area or visited the project, expressed their desire for the castle to collapse. To most, it was a horrific memory of their ancestor's journey en

A view of Cape Coast Castle during its conservation. The cannons faced the ocean, on the left, behind which was a large open platform, and in the upper center, the governor's former residence during the Atlantic Slave Trade. Just below the platform a black door leading to the dungeon where enslaved people were kept until there was transport to the Americas. Ghana, c. 1994.

route to the Americas. They wanted it gone. Many white people felt the opposite, that the castle represented one of the most horrific, but significant, periods in world history—the Trans-Atlantic Slave Trade, the Middle Passage, and the enslavement of Africans in the Americas.

The most notable innovation to the interior space was the creation of the museum with the help of associates from the American Smithsonian Institution. And here was another cross-cultural dilemma: The Castle had originally been a stable for legitimate trade between Africans and Europeans, some of it in European fabrics (subsequently unraveled and rewoven by Ghanaian men), and blown glass beads from Italy, which were traded for Saharan salt and Ashanti gold, among other things. But, from the Ghanaian government's perspective, it was also the site of the first Christian church on the African continent, the location of,the first school, the first government when the British established

Our friend, Edmund, the grandson of Asantehene Prempeh I—a powerful chief of all the Asante people—was a friend and employer of the author, helping develop tours, 1992, in Accra, Ghana.

their supremacy there in the late 1800s, and, finally, very dear to the Ghanaians' heart, the Castle was the base of the first police academy in the country. In their eyes, all of these time-honored institutions deserved equal time and space in the museum.

There was, as you might imagine, a discreet uproar among the American project staff, including from the head of the Smithsonian side of the project, a Jamaican woman of stature. I disagreed vehemently too, but only to Nate since I wasn't part of the project. We felt to a person that The Atlantic Slave Trade, in all its vicious duplicity, extreme inhumaneness and profit-making-agenda, was the most significant, centuries-long ongoing perpetration of repression and destruction to humanity that had ever purposely taken place, until the Holocaust. And it happened here, not only here, but definitely here. Nevertheless, this cross-cultural round was won by the Ghanaians, whose project, Castle, and country it was, after all.

None of the features of the castle elicited the same response from visitors as the dungeon did, but I discuss this in detail in the essay on Panafest. I spent much of my time in Ghana reading as many books as I could get my hands on that related to the Atlantic Slave Trade. I was never able to see any artifacts—whips, manacles, ankle chains or other restraining objects—but I am sure they must have been out there.

I was fortunate to get to know Edmund and Marian, business people and travel agents in Accra. Edmund was the grandson of one of the Kings of the Asante people, known as the Asantehene in Ghana. Neither Edmund, nor his father, could inherit the position of Asantehene. The Asantehene always descended through the maternal line, making it a matrilineal society. The Queen Mothers decided, with the elders, who would become the next Asantehene when the current one passed. Unfortunately, in the late 1800s the British captured one of Edmund's ancestors, Asantehene Prempeh I, kept him and his family under house arrest in Elmina castle, then sent them off to the Seychelles for twenty-four years. The Asantes were fiercely proud and didn't want to lose their culture to the British. They refused to let their children be educated in English, or to attend British schools for a very long time, trying to hang on to their identity. As part of the so-called "Scramble for Africa," the British wanted to do away with the Asante Empire. They even tried to steal their magnificent golden stool.

A very thoughtful and interesting man, Edmund asked me to design some tours, and to assist his staff to become guides for tourists. I tried to do so with the idea that crossing cultures was a two-way street. Tourists, especially, needed to know how to be respectful of Ghanaian cultural norms and traditions. One of the tours I designed was called The Slave Trade Revisited.

The last time I saw Edmund and Marian, was during their first visit to Washington DC, when we were all there. They both worried about being the object of racism as they toured the U.S. It was astonishing to me to think that this grandson of an Asante king and his sophisticated wife had to worry about racism. But then, African Americans had to worry about it all the time.

Our son actually lived the most interesting life in Ghana. After

Our son, Sean, sitting during a school assembly at St. Augustine's College, Cape Coast, where he attended two years of high school, 1990-92.

two weeks in St. Augustine's school, he admitted that it was the people he met, not the buildings, that mattered. And so he would stay. That is not to suggest there weren't difficult moments. This was a boarding school for Ghanaian boys, as well as for those from other parts of West Africa—all 2,000 of them. Sean was the only white student among them, living at home with us. One day an upper classman pulled him aside and said: "Who are you, and what are you doing here?" I can't recall Sean's exact response, but he made a point of giving the young man a fake name.

Sean related stories about how boarders had to bring extra canned food because the meal offerings were meager, and that they sometimes had to get up at three a.m. in order to guarantee a shower in the morning. He soon realized that everyone made an effort to get to class early in order to have a table and a chair. Some of the boys even padlocked them together to assure themselves a place to sit. On occasion the teachers would use a stick to lash the boys for some infringement of the rules. The students would all have to stand in line and await their turn to be lashed. Sean stood in line with them, but he was always pushed aside because he was

Our son, Sean, and four of his good friends in his school class at St. Augustine's College, Cape Coast, Ghana, 1992. When they stayed overnight at our home, they complained of the cold air conditioning.

told that "white boys will bleed to death," if lashed. One day Sean came home and said, "Mom, it happened to me today." I was confused until Sean pulled up the top of his school uniform and showed me the red mark on the small of his back. He was proud to finally be accepted as one of them.

Sean made friends with a group of four guys who spent a lot of time together. They even came to stay the weekend at our house once, but complained about the cold air conditioning. Happy at this school, Sean enjoyed all of his teachers. It took him a while to realize that within the Ghanaian interpretation of British education, he was supposed to take lecture notes and memorize them. Since there were about sixty students in each classroom, no time was allowed for class discussion and no papers were assigned. A bit of a concern among all three of us, we knew that eventually an American college or university would expect experience in class discussions and the writing of papers.

At the end of two years we gave Sean the choice of staying on with us for another two years, or going back to the US to a boarding school to finish high school. It wrenched my heart to think about him being so far away, but we had to give him a choice. By coincidence, the headmaster of Milton Academy visited Ghana and stayed with us for a few days. (Nate had been a student there back in the early 1960s.) In fact, the headmaster actually stayed in an extra bed in Sean's room. He told Sean that he sounded like Milton material and encouraged him to apply. Sean decided finally to apply to three American boarding schools. Based on his experiences living in Ghana, he wrote what was probably one of the most interesting and unusual essays of any applicant that year. Accepted at all three schools, he chose Milton.

At the end of the summer of 1992, after a long and tearful goodbye with Sean at Milton Academy, we returned to Ghana. Twenty-four hours and nearly seven thousand flying miles later, we were back.

ENJOYING GHANA

As we all boogied down the aisle, the choir was singing at full strength, with a drum rhythm that I hadn't heard in a church before. It was time to give our offerings and this is how it was done in the Methodist Church in Cape Coast. Accompanying our neighbor, Emma, we soaked up the warm atmosphere. It was fun to dance in church with everyone dressed in their best African cloth, including us. This kind of boisterous, fun-loving attitude rather defined Ghanaian life. Not that there weren't difficult, sad moments, but most people eventually put a happy, friendly face on it.

As for food, nothing hit the spot like *kofi brokeman*, hot roasted peanuts and plantains, wrapped in newspaper on nearly every street corner. It was the McDonald's of Cape Coast. "Kofi" was the name for a male born on a Friday, and "brokeman" referred to the fact that most men were broke by Friday. (Most Ghanaians from central/south Ghana had formal Christian names, but also day names, by which they were usually called.) Another favorite food often featured at Solace's Restaurant, at the edge of town,

The author holding the new baby, Selorm, belonging to Kwasi (to her right) and Emma (to her left), in Cape Coast, Ghana, 1992 or 1993. Selorm has since graduated from an American college, and is married with two children.

was the popular national dish: *nkatenkwan* with *fufu*. Nkatenkwan was a stew usually made with chicken, tomatoes, eggplant, okra, and ground nuts (peanuts). *Fufu* was made by boiling a mixture of cassava, yam, or plaintain, then pounding it with a mortar and pestle until was a soft dough. The pounding involved two people who alternated rhythmically, moving the glutinous mass around, singing to break up the monotony. Very dangerous work if you could get it. The result was delicious eaten with the stew.

Mostly we ate at home based on the "Triple A plan": African, Asian or American food. I hired a cook who could read recipes allowing our meals to be culturally diverse. On the weekends we ate out, sometimes at places with more familiar western food. We loved eating down the road at an outdoor place on Biriwa Beach, owned by an older Dutch couple who had lived there most of their adult lives. Their chicken cordon bleu was outstanding. But when we felt like steak, the Sanaa Lodge near Sean's school

Nate and Sean at our favorite beach in Ghana, Brenu Beach. It was always peaceful and relaxing to spend time there, c. 1992.

fit the bill. With air conditioning and red velvet curtains, we were temporarily in Great Britain. Nothing like a little Baked Alaska to pull the whole evening off.

As for games, Nate tried tennis at the old tennis club—a fading remnant of British culture—while Sean and I played ping pong inside. Too hot for tennis, in my opinion. Sean tried playing golf on the one dry, blistering hot course outside of town, but it was too much to take and he abandoned his attempts. He also tried playing soccer, the favorite game of Ghanaian boys and men. There was a soccer game going on the school grounds and in open fields almost every day. Even at our home, the neighborhood kids would daily organize an impromptu soccer game on our dirt "lawn." This dirt "lawn" was not intentional. Although we had planted beautiful flowers and grass around the edge of the house, before long the free roaming chickens and goats had eaten it up. We got used to the dirt.

In addition, John, the owner's caretaker of our home, helped us set up a make-do ping pong table with a table made of plywood, and placed it under the roof of our front veranda. We brought

Mustapha Tettey Addy, master drummer (fourth from the left) performing in Kokrobitey's outdoor space, 1993. Note the embroidered leather boots they were wearing, all from the north of Ghana.

back paddles and balls from home. The neighborhood kids loved it, and continued to play even when we weren't around. Eventually all the pieces got lost until the table stood alone.

What we loved most as a family, though, was heading to Brenu beach. The drive west out of town, the turnoff onto a nondescript dirt road, lined with the odd Baobab trees—so iconic in Africa—brought us to Brenu. A remote stunning coastline that glistened in the sunlight, its waves making a soft roar, framed with palm trees, Brenu was the perfect beach. It was wonderful for swimming, body surfing, or just wading. We almost never met anyone there, except people carrying food or kindling on their heads as they walked home to their village. There must have been others who came though, because a woman named Margaret had started a small chop bar, that over the years had gotten a bit more upscale. It was just off the beach, with metal tables and chairs, where we often sat down for some delicious roast chicken and a cold bottle of soda or beer.

We also loved going to Kokrobitey, on the coast near Accra. Master drummer, Mustapha Tettey Addy and his wife, Heidi, had built a wonderful, simple open air resort there. Ghanaian food was served outside while drumming pulsed majestically in the background. Drumming was always accompanied by dancing, I had learned. And Ghanaian drummers, sometimes performing with a natural forked stick, astonished the ears with their multi-rhythmic sounds. After that, it was always easy to identify Ghanaian drumming. Drumming had been at one time a way of communicating among villages, distinctive sounds pounding through the air to tell of arrivals, good news or danger.

Whenever we could get away, we loved traveling to various parts of the country, despite some difficult roads. Since the ocean was south of us, we journeyed, east, north and west. To our north was Kumasi, the center of the brilliant *Asante* culture, the home of the Asantehene. The huge market there had been the largest in West Africa at one time. It was still enormous. In fact, it was easy to get lost as you navigated hundreds of aisles of food, textiles, home goods and African trade beads. These beads interested me a great deal. Created on Murano Island off of Italy, they were traded by

Our son, Sean, learning to play the drums with the drummers at Kokro-bitey, where Mustapha Tettey Addy, master drummer, and his wife, Hei-di, had a drumming school, outdoor performing space, restaurant, and overnight accommodations, 1991.

the Europeans for other goods in what was then The Gold Coast, now Ghana. The beads were created from blown glass and were very intricate, especially the *mille fiore*, and the big blue *chevrons*. Many Asantes still valued them. Chiefs wore them among their gold necklaces and rings. People were buried in them. Many rural villagers believed that beads, which were often found on the ground working their way up from ancient graves, were magically created underground. A particular kind of bead was used to trade for slaves, I had heard, but I never saw one.

I also loved textiles, and the village of Ntonso near Kumasi, was where adinkra cloth was made. Using carved gourds as stamps, these were dipped into a boiling mixture of iron slag and tree bark, then printed onto cotton cloth. Handwoven in former days, adinkra was usually stamped onto commercial white cloth, separate pieces connected by colorful embroidery thread. Adinkra was often called "the goodbye cloth" since it was worn for mourning.

Kente cloth originated in Bonwire, also near Kumasi. Almost every man there was weaving kente strips on their front porch or outside under a tree. I got to know a master weaver named Samuel Cophie. All weavers used portable looms to create their weavings which were easy to move. Kente was only the generic name for a variety of symbolic cloths consisting of woven blocks woven into long narrow strips. The blocks, the designs within them, and the large cloths created from strips—all had symbolic meanings tied to Ghanaian proverbs. When they were sewn together into the finished cloth, they made for the most visually exciting textiles I had ever seen. In an oral culture without a written language, the textiles, proverbs, and drumming were very important ways to convey meaning.

The interesting thing is that men had for centuries been both weavers and sewers of these textiles, in a world where women traditionally did both. I suspected that men might have taken it away from the first weavers, women. When asked why women didn't weave, the answer to me was, women who are pregnant might hurt the fetus by pulling the beater hard against their abdomen when weaving. Originally made from cotton during the Asante's heyday, the kente weaving thrived on unraveled European silk thread. Rayon had since replaced silk.

Ewe kente cloth also thrived in the southeast of Ghana. I got to know one of the finest Ewe weavers in the Volta Region, Gilbert Bobbo Ahiagle. Ewe cloth was usually created from cotton and the designs were simpler than those of the Asante, but lovely. Once we drove there looking to buy antique cloths. Driving there, we discovered what happened when you asked directions. Ghanaian villagers were not familiar with maps, so instead of telling you how to go, they insisted on joining you in the car and taking you there. It was perfectly harmless, and we began to rely on that method because it did the job. In Accra, I was also fortunate to spend some time with Andrew Asare, an Asante weaver whose father had woven a huge piece that hung in the United Nations General Assembly.

We often went to Accra, Nate for business, Sean and I for a change of scenery. Accra had much to offer, but the traffic was forbidding. Although I drove in Ghana, I was afraid to drive to the center of the city. I often took a taxi to the Art Market there, where antique textiles interested me. There were only two fancy hotels in Accra at the time, and one was here in the center, where we could pay to enjoy the pool, and eat a snack in the outside restaurant occasionally. The other was on the opposite side of Accra, on the beach.

We sometimes stayed at the American Club back in Osu, central Accra. We had shunned such clubs in the past, not wishing to spend too much time with expats. But in Accra, the American Club was a cheap place to stay at twenty-five US dollars a night, and even Peace Corps Volunteers were allowed in. That's where we met two Volunteers who were working around Cape Coast, who became "our Peace Corps kids." We loved the Ghanaian staff at the Club, particularly the head bartender, John. My favorite dessert was fruit salad *a la mode*. Otherwise, we enjoyed eating in Lebanese, Chinese, and good Ghanaian restaurants, like Country Kitchens, when in Accra. But we were always eager to get back to Cape Coast.

For our first Christmas in Ghana, our daughter, Windi, and Nate's eighty-year-old mother, flew out to join us. The night before

Cape Coast, Ghana, 1990. Nate's colleague, Kwasi, greeted Nate at our home on Christmas Day as was the Ghanaian tradition.

their arrival, Sean, Nate and I waited until four a.m. for a concert by Ziggy Marley, whose musical instruments had been held up in customs. We could barely get up in the morning, but neither could our first visitors. En route from Accra to Cape Coast we picked up a tropical sort of Christmas tree, it's branches sagging and needles soft. We tied it on top of our car, but when we got home, we saw that it was gone. Nate and Sean turned around and headed back to Accra trying to find it. Amazingly, there it was on the side of the road about half way back. We decorated it as best we could in our wide upstairs hallway.

We had purchased small gifts for everyone, mostly from the Art Market. What we hadn't realized was that Christmas morning was traditionally a time in which Ghanaians visited their friends and extended family. Since we celebrated only with family, it was quite a surprise to see some of Nate's colleagues—Kwasi, Anobil, Dramani and others—come to the door. When New Year's arrived, it was just the opposite: Ghanaians tended to stay home with their

Dramani, one of the drivers on Nate's Cape Coast project, a good man and one of the author's favorite individuals in Ghana, here seen beside our decorated "Christmas tree," Christmas morning, 1990.

family. We were the ones who broke the rules and reached out to them. Cultural differences always played a big role.

While Nate's mother and Windi were with us, we planned a trip next door to the Ivory Coast, for a few days just before New Year's. We loaded our suitcases into the boot and after all five of us squeezed in, seat belts hooked, we took off. Along the way we saw some of the less urban parts of Ghana, as well as the old port city of Takoradi. When we arrived at the border, we were delayed for some time while the officials looked at our passports, perhaps trying to decide what to charge us. Nate's mother, not feeling well, lay down on a bench outside of the customs office. It created such a stir inside that they let us go, no charge. I think they didn't want a white person to die on their watch. Nate's mother recovered, but it was quite an exit.

PANAFEST

The Jamaican Dancers refused to perform. I don't know what happened behind the scenes, but the basic facts were these: Jamaicans were not going to dance on the castle floor, above the graves of their ancestors. The Ghanaians were amazed, appalled, amused—they hadn't been expecting this.

Our lives in Cape Coast had begun about a year before. But on that day we were at Cape Coast Castle, participating in Panafest, held on the giant platform above the dungeons. It was an enormous pan-African festival which welcomed not only African artists, but those from the African Diaspora as well. The issue of the Jamaican Dancers had to be resolved. From the Ghanaian perspective, ancestors took top billing as the most important entities within Ghanaian cultures. Therefore, why wouldn't someone wish to dance on the graves of their ancestors? It was a place fit to celebrate. The Jamaicans, nevertheless, refused to do so. They could not conceive of that transgression. Generously, the Ghanaian coordinators of Panafest agreed to find them a substitute dance floor and they were invited to dance in a performance hall at the university.

All was well on that score, but as an observer to this festival, which went on for days, I couldn't help noticing other cross-cultural currents that no one had anticipated. For example, the British rock group, Public Enemy, were on the bill to perform. As they climbed onto the stage I could tell that the Ghanaians around me were excited to see a well-known and popular band from the West. The first few songs seemed to go well and much applause accompanied the opening numbers. Then, the tide turned when Public Enemy, started to filter into their lyrics, phrases like "Fuck the Queen" and "Fuck the Pope." I looked around: many Ghanaians, both men and women, were covering their mouths in horror, their eyes bright with fear. How could someone say something like that, I could see them thinking. Not even in private would such extreme disrespect be voiced toward either Pope John or Queen Elizabeth. It didn't matter what your religion or nationality was, disrespect towards elders or people in power, was almost unheard of. Strike

Fanti girls at Panafest, in Cape Coast, Ghana. They were dressed in a necklace of beads, plus two pieces of Kente cloth: one rolled across their chest, and the other around their waist down to their ankles, 1992.

A chief dressed in all his gold regalia (some of it gold-painted on wood) and glass beads at Panafest in Cape Coast, 1992.

two, I said to myself. This one didn't get resolved, it just ended when the band jumped offstage and the next performance came on the floor of the Castle.

While events were unfolding inside the Castle, outside there were vendors selling batik shirts and sarongs, kente strips, straw hats and bags, *kentehene* cloth, and beaded jewelry. There were also small carved masks with brass inlay designed only for the tourist trade, since Ghana was one of the few countries in Africa whose cultures didn't use masks. The edible treats the kiosks were selling included fermented *kenkey,* Coca Colas, tiny sweet bananas, and kofi brokeman.

Today, at one of the kiosks, I ran into the Chief of a nearby village, and his wife, both African Americans. He felt that the vendors were working in a sea of chaos, willy nilly, with no thought given to easy access, passageways, or suitable kiosks. Mostly he was annoyed that there were not proper outdoor privies provided for the public. Okay, I thought, another cross-cultural expectation backfired.

About the dungeons themselves, though, there seemed to be no question, no argument. Nothing had ever been done to change the conditions down below. As horrific as it was to contemplate and experience, I was ultimately grateful for that gift of omission.

I had been below before, but during Panafest I went down as often as I could. The African Americans who lived in the nearby village had conceived of and created a tour called "The Door of No Return." Many took that tour, especially those from the Diaspora, but I spent time in the dungeon alone when I could. There were often several people in my vicinity but I was silent, as I knew what to expect and I needed the continual reminder of what happened here. And here was how I experienced this unspeakable place:

A somewhat nondescript double black door opened off of the upper platform of the enormous castle. The brilliantly blue sky and slow sailing clouds above, along with the narrow fishing boats entering the crashing surf nearby, blinded my initial descent over a long ramp to the hell below, invisible in its blackness, just as it had been when enslaved persons were imprisoned here. Luckily, the lights were suddenly turned on, at the switch near the entrance, and I slowly navigated down, afraid to trip and fall onto this mound of stuff that made up the floor, still there after centuries. Nearby Elmina Castle's dungeon floor had been cleaned up for visitors, but not this one. It proved that people had actually existed here. This floor was no doubt a foot thick, a combination of all the body fluids and excreta that emerged from both life and death: saliva, phlegm, vomit, tears, flakes of dead skin, fingernails, toenails, semen, menstrual blood, the blood and fluids of wounds and infections, placentas, urine, feces. I could hardly bear to visualize it all.

I moved to my right where there was a room, perhaps 20 feet by 30 feet, blank walls except for a small air vent on the ocean side. When I went left I walked through two more small rooms, of no more than fifteen by twenty feet, which led me down even further into the depths. I remember that I had once been below when the lights were suddenly turned off and the result was a darkness like I had never experienced before, but one in which enslaved persons had lived. Here, even with the light on I felt myself visualize all its negative manifestations. The fetid air. The sordid molestation. The running feces. The non-potable water. The inedible food. All done to innocent Black people in dark anonymity.

Finally, I was in the last room at the end. I looked back through the murky air, the half dark space and realized that all the rooms together probably crowded perhaps a thousand slaves at any one time. There in front of me, fittingly, was a shrine to which people had brought gifts over the years. These gifts were mainly from Ghanaians, representing their belief in spirits and related talismans, odd bones and shells, carved figures and beads. I was touched that they chose to remember those who were sold away. But afterwards I had to prepare myself to imagine the most difficult part of this whole involuntary journey. The long hallway leading out of the dungeon was blocked.

I could not experience the interminable walk to the Middle Passage across the Atlantic that those who survived took. I had to go outside a different way, through the sunshine and fragrant air to an iron gate. That was the 'Door of No Return'. From this exact place, there was no turning back. Canoes had taken the enslaved persons, crowded in random configurations, without care for relationships or children, over rough surf to the waiting vessels some distance off shore. From there they were chained to the floor of the ship for most of the journey to the Americas, to a life and work that was as yet inconceivable. Finally, paradoxically relieved and weighted down at the same time, I exited the Castle.

Why did I describe this terrible journey below Cape Coast Castle while I attended Panafest? Because it was the Castle's most difficult, infamous story, and because this is where Panafest played out on its surface. Without the Castle, the subsequent Atlantic Slave Trade and the great African Diaspora that followed, along with many of the performances at the festival wouldn't have, couldn't have, occurred. Neither would the conservation of Cape Coast Castle have been undertaken, nor what happened there been as viscerally remembered. So, there was a connection, a significant connection, to Panafest. Subsequently for me this story and its ramifications became almost an obsession. I knew practically nothing about The Atlantic Slave Trade. Where was it in our history books, beyond a mention? Now I knew why I was here and what I needed to pursue.

ENCOUNTERS WITH ARMED OFFICERS IN GHANA

Some of the encounters we experienced in Ghana were with the police or military. They were unpredictable, not because the officers were violent, but because they often needed money or a ride. Like many other government employees at the time, they weren't paid enough. So when they met an obroni on the road they typically asked for a *dash*, meaning a little money on the side, extra cash. They would sometimes stop you for no apparent reason, question you, and sometimes get in your car. At those times it was a little scary.

On one occasion, we had welcomed Sean back from the States for a visit and we had balloons in the car. For no apparent reason, at Kotoka Airport a military person stopped us. He had questions which I cannot now remember. But the result was that he got into our car. As soon as the officer sat down a balloon popped. There was momentary confusion, as he tried to figure out what had happened and how to proceed. Nate and I sat in place, frozen with alarm. Sean turned to tell the officer we had done nothing wrong, but Nate gently pulled Sean back. Nothing further happened as we rode around Accra for several minutes. Finally, the officer asked for an outrageous dash and we negotiated, then gave him some money as he finally got out of the car.

Once I started driving the two hours from Cape Coast to Accra and back on my own, I usually felt fairly safe as I passed the checkpoint half way through. Always, the police would ask for something for their Christmas Box. I usually responded with a smile, indicating it wasn't yet Christmas, and gave them a small dash. On one such trip, I was stopped at the checkpoint and two police officers with AK47s asked me to pull over. I couldn't figure out what was happening. Then they asked if they could get a ride to Cape Coast. Did I have a choice?

The police officers got in the back seat, with their AK47s facing the car's roof. We had another thirty miles or so to go. Neither of us said anything as we moved through the countryside. Gradually I started to feel more confident, less scared. The police didn't have many vehicles to spare across the country. They just needed a ride, period. So, when we reached the circle just before Cape Coast, they asked to get down, thanked me in Fanti, and I drove away, smiling to think of the story I was going to tell Nate and Sean.

Then, one early morning in our Cape Coast home, Sean ran into our bedroom to say we had been burglarized. Nate and I immediately got up to see what he was talking about. In the wide hall between our bedrooms, an antique kente cloth draped on the wall, our CD/cassette player and all of our music, plus various small items, were missing. While I was wondering how this could have happened, I noticed that the glass louvers from one of the windows facing the big balcony had been carefully removed and laid on a lawn chair outside. That was how they had entered the house. But how had they gotten to the second floor? John, the house owner's caretaker, had obviously been asleep on the veranda below.

We immediately got John and Evans, the young man who worked for us, together to try to figure this out. We asked if anyone they knew might have asked questions, or if they had noticed anyone checking out our house. No one could come up with any leads. So we reported it to the police, knowing that this was probably the end of it, because their resources were not large and this burglary was comparatively small.

A few days later, much to our surprise, Nate received a note, asking him to come down to the police station. He was informed that someone had escaped the local jail just before our house was burglarized. They had a couple of CDs to show him, which were ours. They had the burglar in custody again. Nate returned home to tell us the news. We were all grateful but not sure what would happen next.

A few weeks later, Nate was told that he needed to take a trip to Takoradi with the police. They also asked him to drive because they had no vehicle. So, Nate drove to Takoradi with two policemen in the back seat, and the handcuffed burglar between them. Together they all went to a hearing before a judge. Nate identified our objects—amazingly all of them had been found. Afterwards, he drove everyone back to Cape Coast and the burglar was put back in jail. Soon, we restored the antique kente cloth to our wall again, plus our CD/cassette player and all of our music returned to our upstairs hall. Life was back to normal.

A GHANAIAN FUNERAL

I had been surprised to see liquor being poured on the floor of the balcony outside our hotel room on our first night in Ghana. I later learned that a libation was done for important occasions: the birth of a child, a special project, and the celebration of a life. So, a libation was very much a part of a funeral too. Even though the German Schnapps, now produced in Ghana, was a favorite libation—wine or water could also be used. At a funeral a libation honored the deceased as they joined the ancestors. It was essentially an offering to the ancestral spirits. They were always present.

Funerals were actually an important part of a Ghanaian's life, as odd as that sounds. From a Ghanaian's perspective, the most significant transition in a person's life was, ironically, their death. It was the one time when thousands of *cedis* would be raised and spent for the occasion. Money was needed to keep the body safe in a cold storage for possibly months, for the printing of pamphlets, posters and newspaper announcements. And, finally, for the occasion itself, to pay for "official" mourners, food and plenty of drink, the rental of a bed for the deceased, among other expenses. In the old days without electricity, bodies deteriorated quickly, and funerals had to happen soon, even without elaborate fundraising or fancy events. This was probably still true in small villages, but not in the cities.

Religion was important too. About half of all Ghanaians were Christians, but it was Christianity with African overtones. The famous Archbishop Peter Sarpong, wrote a book showing how Christianity and African religion had much in common. They both believed in a God, which helped the overlap. The most famous Adinkra symbol, referring to proverbs, was the *Gye Nyame* sign. It looked like the fingers of a person's two fists grabbing each other, with the thumbs released in both hands. It meant that "without God we are nothing" or that 'God is omnipotent." This proverb helped us grasp the Ghanaians attitude towards death.

When we were in Ghana, some craftsmen also began to make a significant impact on funerals, at least for those of some wealth. An Accra artist had begun making special caskets at the request of the family of the deceased. The casket could have been at the request of the deceased before his or her death as well. These caskets were created in the shape of something the individual liked–a pink Cadillac, chili peppers, a pair of shoes, a banana, etc. These extraordinary caskets were carefully carved from wood and painted in bright colors. The carved interior of the casket was laid out with tufted satin for a comfortable ride to the land of the ancestors.

Above all, funerals were celebrations of a long life. This kind of celebration didn't happen for young children who hadn't lived long enough to become adults. At one point we were able to take part in a funeral, when a driver for the United Nations project had a fatal car accident. It was certainly unfortunate—and sad—for those who knew and cared for him, his family, friends, and colleagues. A couple of months later we all gathered to celebrate his life.

Our son Sean, now fifteen years old, didn't want to go. He had never seen a dead body before, so we said he should just come for the celebration. We were dressed in western clothes, dark brown and blue. Most of the other male celebrants wore large toga like cloths made from adinkra, in dark red and black. Adinkra cloths were always hand printed with symbols representing cultural proverbs. The women traditionally wore *kaba* and *slit* (form fitting long sarongs and a blouse) in commercial African cloth, sometimes with printed Adinkra symbols, in dark colors.

Before we knew it we were moving in a long line of celebrants leading to the bed where the deceased lay. Sean stayed in line because he was obviously curious, just a little afraid of what he might see. Soon the body came into view, laid on a decorative Victorian iron bed. The body was dressed, sporting bracelets of trade beads and gold necklaces glistening in the artificial light, on a series of pillows and covered in beautiful cloths, sometimes kente, or maybe commercial pink eyelet. Around him were a bevy of official mourners hired for the occasion. All women, the mourners sobbed and yelled in their pretended sorrow, waving handkerchiefs in the air.

When we all came out of the room of the dead, a priest performed a libation in honor of the UN driver, enabling him to join the ancestors. There was no fancy casket. Lots of music, dancing and drumming followed, to help the deceased on his journey. The celebration of life had begun. Long tables were covered with Ghanaian cooked dishes, cakes, tropical fruits, and nuts. Local beers, palm wine, and European wines cooled in ice-filled bins. And, of course, there was Schnapps.

ACCRA, GHANA: THE AMBASSADORS' SPECIAL SELF-HELP PROGRAM, 1993-1994

Our daughter, Windi, a new college graduate, took off full speed ahead with our old car, plus a check in her hand to begin life as an adult. And we flew off to Ghana again, but this time I had a job: the coordinator for the American Ambassador's Special Self-Help Program. I was excited to start. But it meant trying to find a place for me to stay in Accra, at least part of the time. I was lucky because an American family departing for Kenya said I could rent their house for about $100 a month. Seemed fair to me.

I had met the American Ambassador several times. To me he seemed very accessible, not standing on protocol—at least not all the time. His wife, Bonnie, was also very present and visible in Ghana and one of the first women to join my cross-cultural women's group in Accra. She also started a Ghanaian Bead Society, to make sure antique trade beads, as well as relatively newer Ghanaian powdered glass beads, were conserved in the museum. I liked them both.

The American Ambassador introducing the President of Ghana, behind him, Jerry John Rawlings, before the latter made a speech, near Cape Coast, Ghana, c. 1993.

I am not sure how I got this job at the Embassy—apparently it was open to non-diplomatic Americans like me—but this was my first time to physically go inside. I had been very shocked over the years at how American Embassies had become veritable fortresses. I knew this had developed along with fears of terrorism. In any case, the one in Accra was moderately protected in 1993. Still I had to park outside, walk up to a gatehouse, give my name and mission to the Ghanaian guards and show my passport. They would then call the Marine Guard in the Embassy or one of the offices to see if I had an appointment. After I got the job, the differences were only slightly altered: I was let through the gate to the inside parking lot after showing my Embassy ID. Then I had to walk across that lot of blazing hot white stone gravel to my new office in the library attached to the Embassy. My office was not in the embassy proper, but connected. Each time I wanted to go see the Ambassador, I had to go through the Marine Guard, who called his office. You get the picture.

Although Nate had worked for many years in economic development in various countries where we lived, I hadn't taken it on myself. I had little background, so I first read all the files of pending applicants from village leaders. These village groups had to have started a project for the entire community's benefit, but were unable to continue when their money ran out. I have no idea how these villagers ever learned about this program, but we had many applicants. Sometimes they would come unannounced to the Ghanaians in the Guard House outside the wall, wishing to talk with me. The guards would call me occasionally, though mostly they would tell them to make an appointment first. But sometimes I would go outside and meet with them. I was amazed at how roughly the guards often treated their own countrymen. I guess they felt empowered being associated with this Embassy. Or maybe they were just following orders.

The applications were for everything from shea butter production, to the building of latrines, and the collection of trees to produce telephone poles. It seemed very unfair that telephone wires could only be connected when villagers had collected enough

The author, son Sean, and husband Nate, visiting and paying respects to villagers in northern Ghana, while coordinating the Ambassador's Special Self-Help Program, 1994.

poles to carry them. But Ghana was still relatively poor, and most people had no access to phones. In fact, although we were relatively well off in a small city, we had no phone at our home for the four years we lived in Cape Coast. The bird I heard at night outside our bedroom window sounded like a phone ringing, an amazing tease. We spent about six hundred US dollars a month on hour long calls from Nate's office to our kids back in the States.

Meanwhile, when I had eventually decided on several applications to put forward to the Ambassador, a committee was called together to hear my presentation. This included the Peace Corps director, and representatives from a couple of NGO's working in development. All I remember from the first such meeting was how I was shot down by the Peace Corps director: six latrines for a village of 1500 was not enough. So much for that application.

The best part of the job was an opportunity to visit some of these sites. I arranged for a visit up to the northwest of Ghana, very rural, in a part of the country I had never seen. Fortunately, it coincided with the spring high school vacation break of my son, Sean. I invited Nate and Sean to come with me. I had been given a car, Chevrolet Suburban brand, and a Ghanaian driver to take us from village to village. The driver drove ahead of us and met us in Kumasi where we had flown. Along the way we stayed in small hotels or guest houses, some very clean, some never appeared to have been cleaned. But we had no choice, we took what was available.

Visiting with the villagers was a delight as they were obviously happy to see us. I had sent out letters to each one weeks before, advising them that I would be coming with my son and husband. The first village presented my son with a child's hand woven shirt. Unfortunately, Sean was now eighteen and 6'2", but he tried it on anyway, to everyone's amusement. How could they have known? This was a village where they manufactured Shea butter from the Shea nut, readily available here. This butter was very much in demand in the West for cosmetics and soap, so the project was bound to produce an income for the village.

We visited villages asking for help with squat latrines and wells too, sometimes along with Peace Corps Volunteers working in those villages. While there, we were entertained with local food, drumming and dancing. We appreciated the time and effort, not to mention the expense, that this kind of hospitality entailed. We enjoyed meeting all the village leaders and learned a lot about their projects so that I was able to return to Accra better informed. Our driver became our interpreter when our southern Ghana Fanti language skills would not suffice.

While there, we were able to spend a night at one of the two major national parks in Ghana, the other one being Kakum National Park, which Nate was working on near Cape Coast. This one was called Mole National Park. It was huge, some one million acres or so. We were only able to visit small parts of it, but the reason for going there was primarily to see elephants. These elephants were smaller than those in East Africa, and there were no big safaris carried out in Ghana. But the opportunity to see wildlife was always a treat.

After about a week, we ended up in Bolgatanga, a very different northern city. People here made their houses from mud and decorated their exteriors with painted designs. They also made beautiful baskets, with colored stripes that became very popular in the US. We were practically on the northern border of Ghana, next to Burkina Faso. Sean was very disappointed that we didn't go over the border. Instead, we started back to Kumasi on perhaps the roughest road we had yet encountered. It was paved but full of huge potholes. It took us almost ten hours to go less than three hundred miles in our huge Chevrolet Suburban. Fortunately for me, I was able to sit in the front with the driver (it was my job, after all.) So I was relatively comfortable, holding onto the bar above the door, while Sean and Nate spread their hands on the car ceiling to protect their head from the impact of the potholes. After a long day, we arrived back in Kumasi, following the most interesting trip I ever took in Ghana.

DIRECTING AN AFRICAN ARTS AND CULTURE PROGRAM, 1995-1997

For our son Sean's senior year, we went to the U.S., renting an apartment in Milton, Massachusetts, so that we could watch his games, meet his teachers, see him off to the senior prom in his rented tux and rented limo, and, of course, watch him graduate from Milton Academy.

While there, I learned of a position opening up in Ghana, with the School for International Training's Semester Abroad program. I applied and drove up to Brattleboro, Vermont, to be interviewed. I think my four years in Ghana, and active interest in arts and culture got me the job. I was to start the following August. In the meantime, Nate had applied for a Fulbright research fellowship, in an effort to better understand the connection between Ghanaian culture and business practices. He was accepted too. We had both found new ways to continue our engagement with Ghana.

My co-director was a Nigerian man named Yemi. We got along well, and together with Nate, the three of us rented a house in the northern part of Accra. We borrowed furniture from Nate's colleague, Kwasi, while he was building his own house. SIT

The author's co-director, Yemi, sitting with a student from the SIT program, in Accra, Ghana, probably 1995. The author and her husband lived with Yemi quite happily together in a house rented by SIT.

provided a desk and phone. It was pretty spartan but suited us just fine. The only problem was driving to the house in our old car. The potholes were so big in the dry season that you could get lost in them. And, in the wet, muddy season, it was almost impossible to navigate. Somehow we managed.

That initial semester I was extremely nervous waiting for the first students to arrive. As usual, all the flights came close to midnight, and we took the fifteen or so exhausted students to vacant dorm rooms at the University of Ghana in nearby Legon. The next day we began the semester focused on experiential learning across the country, language training, and independent studies. It was an exciting prospect.

There were always more women than men. I thought that was probably because parents felt a structured college program was safer for the women. But I found that women were often even more curious than the men, and sometimes able to connect better with the culture and people. In any case, one of the first things we did was to discover the subject of independent study each student wanted. That way we could begin to help arrange it. One of my

The author with a group of SIT students and Ghanaian men during a field trip in Tamale, northern Ghana, 1996.

first students said she would like to study Ghanaian masks. She didn't yet know that Ghanaians didn't use masks.

Over the course of a semester, the students listened to Ghanaian drumming, talked to village chiefs, learned to dance *ajowa*, watched men weaving kente strips, helped women pound fufu, listened to master drummer, Mustapha Tettey Addy, perform at Kokrobitey, sat in on university lectures on Ghanaian history or economics, and so much more. We also drove all over the country to see what Ghana looked like and how the culture changed as we moved.

One of our first destinations was the Central Region along the coast, the home of both Cape Coast and Elmina castles. There the Portuguese, Dutch, English and other European nations had lived one after another over the centuries. In fact, Elmina Castle, the oldest, built in 1482 by the Portuguese, had been visited by Christopher Columbus. In 1492, legend has it that he set his compass against the one on the castle's grounds, before heading to the Americas. Exuding so much history to process and absorb, as I mentioned earlier, these castles had been a major part of the Atlantic Slave Trade. We always had two or three African Americans each semester, and they saw the dungeons as incredibly personal and traumatizing for them. I chose to stay close to give comfort, sometimes accepted, sometimes not. I was aware of the irony of a white American trying to help a black American, when faced with the tragedy of the Atlantic Slave Trade, begun by greedy white Europeans.

We always took a long bus ride to Kumasi, watching life along the highway with baskets, red palm oil, and shea butter on view to buy. We managed to meet with the son of the Asantehene in his palace, and viewed the first floor museum. We witnessed the place where, in 1701, a priest named Akomfo Anokye—the sidekick of the first Asantehene, Osei Tutu—empowered a golden stool to emerge from the heavens, during a thunderstorm. That was the legend believed by all Asantes. Akomfo Anokye also plunged a sword into the ground to claim the place, Kumasi, for the Asante people. Astoundingly, the sword was still stuck in the earth, clearly visible on the modern hospital grounds of Kumasi. The threat was that if anyone ever pulled it out, the Asante's power would end, also true of a small leather bag of unknown items in the Kumasi museum. None of us were about to trifle with those possibilities.

After a few weeks of *twi* language training in Kumasi, along with homestays among families, we always headed farther north to Tamale. There the culture, language and religion changed. Most of the Ghanaians in the south and central part of the country had converted to Christianity, beginning as far back as the Portuguese. Most Northerners were people who identified with Islam. In contrast to their male counterparts in southern Ghana, the men traditionally wore—not big twelve-foot kente cloths draped over one shoulder like a toga—but oversized handwoven embroidered striped shirts and baggy pants. Sometimes the shirts had small

The hilt of the sword plunged into the earth on a hill claimed for the Asante people by Akomfo Anokye, the priest of the chief, Osei Tutu, in 1701, which became, Kumasi, Ghana. The sword hilt was still there on the later hospital grounds, 1997.

leather shields on them, symbols of protection from past battles. The countryside was dry and nearly flat, as we drove across the grassy *savanna*, just below the *sahel* and the Sahara Desert. From here the dust that caused the *harmattan* began annually, like a fine mist flowing down to the coast.

For the most part, the students were terrific. At first they identified more with me, another American, and later they began identifying more with Yemi, as they grew accustomed to Ghana. Over time, this included a few gay students whom we had to warn not to act on their sexual instincts. In Ghana, there was a law against homosexual activity. We didn't want to see any of our students in jail.

On a lighter note, some students had a hard time not getting eggs and buttered toast for breakfast, or hamburgers and French fries for lunch. A few didn't take their anti-malaria pills and got malaria. Fortunately, they recovered, as did others who drank local water in plastic bags, and got diarrhea and cramps. But they all learned from Ghana, as we continued to as well.

On one bus ride back from Tamale, I was sitting up front with Yemi. It was our usual spot so we could compare notes, count our cedis, and plan ahead. We had put a big box of bottled water in the aisle of the bus for the students, the bus driver and for Yemi and me to drink as we drove through suffocating heat. Another box for empty bottles sat there too. We offered water to the driver, but, as he continued to throw his empty bottles out the window, I finally spoke to Yemi. We agreed we should ask the driver to throw his bottles into the box, instead of out the window. He was happy to do that. But at the end of the trip before we hit Accra, the driver stopped the bus momentarily to throw the whole box of empty

The author dancing to "The Western Diamonds" band in Ghanaian dress for one of the SIT parties celebrating the end of a semester, at Country Kitchens' restaurant, Accra, Ghana, probably 1997.

water bottles out of the bus, into the weeds beside the highway. A cultural misunderstanding if ever there was one.

MACEDONIA

Former Yugoslav Republic of Macedonia

Our cat, Stormy, resting on the wall hanging representing "Integration of Cultural Differences" that I created as part of a series of wall hangings based on Dr. Milton Bennett's "Developmental Model of Cultural Sensitivity." in Skopje, Macedonia, 2006.

SKOPJE, MACEDONIA

I commented to a few of Nate's project colleagues that we had never lived in Europe before, Macedonia was our first time. Practically in unison, they said: "This is not Europe. This is the Balkans." Apparently Macedonians saw themselves as very much separate from Europe, by which they meant western Europe. I couldn't see it at first, given that there were tall, long-legged young women walking around in leather mini-skirts, salad (*shopska salata*) was practically the national dish, and coffee bars were everywhere. None of this existed in Asia or Africa when we lived there.

It was 2006. Somewhat controversially, the independent republic of Macedonia had been created from the former southern state of Yugoslavia, after its demise. The Greeks refused to recognize it. Ancient Macedonia had covered parts of both countries, supposedly the home of Alexander the Great, though Bulgarians often claimed him as well, because the borders overlapped at one point. The Romans had been here too, as evidenced by the remains of ancient aqueducts and temples. Then the Ottoman Empire reigned over Macedonia for more than five hundred years, until the early twentieth century. The impact of this was still remembered by many people in Macedonia. They referred to it as "The Ottoman Yoke."

Skopje, the capital, was composed mainly of ethnic Macedonians, who had their own Macedonian Orthodox Church; the ethnic Albanians who were mostly Muslim; and the Roma, who, by and large, owned very little, but many were Muslims.

Nate had accepted a job for only a year, replacing someone who became ill during a USAID project. For the first time overseas, we lived on the seventh floor of a downtown apartment building in Skopje. Most of the eight floors were divided into two halves. The eighth floor was taken up entirely by the family of a famous national athlete, whom we never met. A two-person elevator brought us up to our apartment. In actuality, two people could go up empty-handed, or one person with groceries could go up alone, the other taking the stairs. An old building, but situated next to the President's building, and close to Nate's office, made the location very convenient. More importantly, it was beside the lovely Vardar River, across from which was a castle and the old Ottoman town called *Carsija*. There, the old Turkish baths, inns and stables, had been converted to restaurants and art galleries. It was said that the Ottomans built these original amenities every forty miles or so, determined by the length of a horse's average daily ride.

Our apartment was roomy—two bedrooms, two bathrooms, an office and an open living room/kitchen. A series of windows faced the west and the rest of the city. On a small outdoor balcony we could eat and watch the neighbors get ready for work or have dinner in their apartments across the street. We often saw a family of Roma in the street below us, on their wagon pulled by a horse, calling out for metal or glass refuse.

We had brought a pet overseas for the first time: an older cat named Stormy. She managed the nearly sixteen hours in transit between airports and flying, in a small carrier. We almost made it through Macedonian customs without anyone noticing her, but in the end we declared her and had her two chips checked out. On the first night in our new-to-us apartment, Stormy got loose. Frightened, I searched for her, but couldn't find her until the following morning, hiding behind some potted plants on the floor below. Other than that incident, she spent a lot of time looking out our windows, and only once escaped to the balcony unsupervised.

Meanwhile, as a result of claiming Stormy upon our arrival at the airport, for the next four weeks I was visited by a gentleman—looking much like I imagined a Russian KGB officer would look—who stopped by our apartment, examined Stormy, and took notes. It was a silent visit, as neither of us were able to speak each other's language. The visits stopped abruptly without explanation.

Living in the city center was a first for us. Most of the buildings reminded us of old communist Russia: very simple and concrete. We didn't have a car, but could borrow the project car to travel in-country on the weekends. So we walked almost everywhere in Skopje, although just getting across the street could be very dangerous. We bought a bike, one that we could share on alternate days. A wonderful seven-kilometer bike path looped along the river. It was a joy to ride on it and be in the outdoors. But the air was, in fact, the only serious problem for me. Skopje sat in a valley among mountains, and Mount Vodno towered over the city's western edge, lit at the top by a giant cross. This meant that the valley air was fairly concentrated. Unfortunately for me, Skopje was literally heated by a central heating system that used coal, which didn't do much for my asthma.

In all other ways, our year of living in Macedonia was wonderful. Because our children were grown and away, we could immerse ourselves in it freely while still enjoying visits by Windi, Sean and his new wife, Nancy. We loved going to the open air markets, even though many vegetables and fruits were unrecognizable. Striding through the luxurious supermarkets, we didn't always understand what we were buying there either. But because eating in restaurants was so good and so relatively inexpensive, we ate out a lot. Each meal began with a huge shopska salata, covered in grated white cheese, meant to be accompanied by *rakjia*, Macedonian brandy. My favorite dishes were *tavce gravce* (a bean dish), *burek* (a spinach/cheese pie), *pastrmalija* (pizza) and *moussaka*, sometimes ending with a sweet *baklava*, which was endemic to the whole region.

I loved looking at old textiles and discovered a small shop down the street from our apartment—a mixed bag of *kilims*, costumes, interesting artifacts and junk. The door was locked, but the first time I knocked, the shopkeeper came rushing across the street with the key. When there were no customers he would always be sipping espresso at a café opposite, looking out the window. Each time I visited, once I got his attention, he showed me several beautiful antique kilims and eventually I bought two to bring home.

The author's neighbor, Danica, actress and good friend in Skopje, Macedonia, met while she was sweeping her stoop across the hall from our apartment in 2006.

Because our contract was only for a year we made the most of it. Now quite experienced in finding language teachers and forming cross-cultural women's groups, I was off and running within a month. As a couple, we traveled weekends to every nook and cranny of this small country, sometimes more than once. The small town of Ochrid, and its lake arising from the fresh spring in its center, was a favorite. We ate in little restaurants on the water, stayed in small inns, and twice in a former monastery. Staying in the monastery was unique, if cold. With visiting friends as the only guests both times, we enjoyed comfortable rooms and some good food, while being warmed by tiny coal stoves in the dining room. From the small chapel on the grounds, the soft recordings of medieval chants quietly announced themselves.

It took a while to get to know people, given the language barrier. Early on, I stepped out of my apartment and across the hall a beautiful woman was sweeping her stoop. We greeted each other tentatively, because at the time I spoke only English. But she knew a little English, introduced herself as Danica, and invited me into her apartment. This apartment, a near replica of ours, was astonishingly modern and stunning by comparison. Everything was in black and white, including the leather sofas. On the shelf of the back wall were religious icons and below that, several guitars set on stands. She indicated that she had two children, both teenagers. Her husband, Petar, was a musician and Danica, herself, was an actress. She was also a wonderful cook and over time we enjoyed several great Macedonian meals in her home, surrounded by her family and friends. On one evening, they also took us to a wonderful restaurant with live music, in which we reveled. Danica became my first good friend in Macedonia, and she introduced me to many others. I also introduced her to my very artistic Armenian friend, Mine, who was the wife of Nate's Macedonian colleague, Jane. I was happy that they subsequently became close friends.

The author's good friend, Mine, an artist from Armenia, married to Jane, Nate's colleague on the USAID project, in Skopje, Macedonia, 2006.

I had arrived with an idea for a personal project in Macedonia. Having been a fiber artist in my earlier adult life, I decided to spend some time here creating a series of fabric wall pieces. I had been collecting fabrics my entire time living overseas. Those I brought to Skopje were scraps leftover from clothes sewn in each country in which we had lived. My goal was to assemble scraps so that they abstractly symbolized the several stages individuals often experienced while learning to live in other cultures.* I had experienced many of these stages myself, in various countries. To make the wall pieces simple and effective, I decided to cut the scraps into triangles, so that sewn together they could show direction. Then I went to a local hardware store in Skopje and picked up a seven-foot countertop, which Nate set up against the western windows of our apartment, supporting it with a couple of saw horses. In a fabric store I purchased different colored linen fabrics for the background of each wall piece. I bought stretcher strips, making frames to stretch the background fabrics onto, and secured them with heavy duty staples. Lastly, I set up my sewing machine, and sewed together double sided triangles. Then I arranged directional patterns with the similarly colored triangles for each wall piece. The project was off to a good start.

A day before our departure, I realized that I hadn't collected any scraps of fabric from Macedonia. I had the kilims, but I wasn't about to cut these up. So, I went back to my friend, the shopkeeper, and asked if he had any small scraps of fabrics I could have. He paused for a moment, thinking, then disappeared into a back room for five minutes while I waited. Finally, he came out and handed me an old plastic bag full of scraps. I thanked him, he wished me well, and I said goodbye for the last time.

Nearly five a.m. on Christmas Eve I hugged my good friend and neighbor, Danica, farewell. Nate and I made several trips down the two-person elevator, stuffed our bags into the waiting company car, and departed for the airport.

*See the essay "Getting to Know a Place and Its People" (page 227) for a full description of the stages of cultural sensitivity from ethnocentric to ethno-relative.

SUMNAL: THE ROMA CENTER IN MACEDONIA

Early in 2006, I walked by a large warehouse in Skopje with my language teacher, who informed me that thousands of Roma had been killed there during the Holocaust. I was shocked. I had, naively, not realized that Roma had been part of the Nazi genocide of Jews during World War II. Roma were formerly known as Gypsies, because some thought that they had been slaves in Egypt at one time, although that was never proved. The term gypsy had been considered very pejorative for some time. The Roma most likely migrated from Northern India approximately a thousand years ago and spoke an Indo-Aryan language. They traveled around Europe, and, to some extent the US, often very poor, and sometimes became known as thieves. They continued to be discriminated against. But a large area

The Roma kids from the Sumnal Center on a cultural excursion with the author in Skopje, Macedonia. The Roma woman on the left was Fatma, the director of the program, and in the center, Elez, her assistant who became a good friend, 2006.

of Skopje, known as Suto Orizari, or Shutka, was considered the biggest self-ruled Roma district in Europe, consisting of a population of several thousands. There they lived freely speaking Romani. I was still new to Skopje and had a lot to learn.

The next day Nate came home from work and talked about his visit to Sumnal, a center to support the education of Roma children. He said I might want to visit. So I called Fatma, the head of the Center, and made an appointment to come visit the following afternoon. Fatma greeted me in excellent English, along with Elez, a teacher there who also spoke English. They said they were encouraging the Roma children to go to school with the ethnic Macedonian children. Suffering prejudice from other ethnic groups in the country, most of the parents had never been to school. Sumnal offered a pre-school program. They also helped the parents learn ways to support their kids. For the older students, Sumnal held an after school program assisting them with their homework and offering enrichment programs. I was very impressed with the entire Center.

Fatma had been fortunate to have achieved a college degree and spoke impeccable English. I am certain she had worked very hard for that status. I was not sure how Elez had learned English, but his fluency was remarkable. I observed that he related very well to the kids, and seemed to have street smarts too. Towards the end of my visit, Fatma said they were looking for a volunteer to offer after-school arts programs for the older kids. I held up my hand and said, "Yes!" Right up my alley, I couldn't wait to begin.

I decided to start with drawing, for the dozen or so thirteen to fifteen-year-old kids, and we got out paper and markers. I urged them to try to draw each other's profiles, and gave them some guidelines. The results were amusing to them. Another time we rolled out the white butcher paper and cut off pieces for entire body lengths. Then each person lay down on the paper and someone else drew around them with a pencil, to lots of laughs. That person then had to color in the outline with his or her own hair, features and clothes. Afterwards we hung them around the room, as we did every time I visited.

Eventually, I bought some stretcher strips and nails, along with balls of heavy string. I helped each student put together a frame with nails across the top and bottom, from which we wound the string as a warp for weaving. We started with tearing off strips of paper from old magazines, and I showed them how to create a weft going over and under the warp strings. Next we tried weaving with strips of cloth I had brought from home. And finally, we used yarns from my collection, so that they could learn to make simple tapestries for wall hangings. They were pleased with the results. I was loving it.

Over the course of the year, I began to venture beyond the walls of the Sumnal Center with the students. With permission and help from Fatma and Elez, I took the students to central Skopje, where some of them had never been. I knew virtually nothing of the Romani language, and although I was learning Macedonian, I was not fluent. Still, among us, we made fun things happen. Together we went to a small restaurant near my apartment and I said they could order whatever they wanted. They chose Cokes, French fries and pizza mostly. The next time we got together, we visited a high school, where other Roma students had a small band, with violin, saxophone, drums and flute. It was fun for the Sumnal kids to see what some of their peers were doing, and inspiring for them to listen. The following week I learned there was a circus performing not far from Sumnal. Though not overly interested in circuses myself, the kids were excited to see animals and people performing in ways they had not seen before. And they were always gracious in thanking me for what we did together.

At some point I was able to figure out more enriching experiences for them. Luckily, I was able to get discounted tickets for them at the symphony. How I did this with my limited language skills, I can't remember. I am sure that none of the students had ever been to the symphony. It was an evening performance and we took three or four taxis to get there. Our discounted tickets provided only back row seats, which were probably not the best, but they listened, at least to the first half.

The author working with Roma students who were making a wall hanging at the Sumnal Center, Skopje, Macedonia, 2006.

When they got fidgety, we decided we should not push our luck. At least they had been exposed.

One of our last trips into town was to a concert of traditional Macedonian music and dance. I had already seen performances of the National Ensemble for Dances and Songs of Macedonia. I was in contact with the director of that company, which was called Tanec. I asked if we could bring Roma students to a concert for free and he agreed. So, on the afternoon in question, we loaded everyone into taxis once again and took off for the concert venue. It was very exciting for them to see the costumes, the various instruments, and the dances. It was thrilling music more familiar to them than that of the symphony. They also got to sit in the front row and I could see the awe and happy interest on their faces. Near the start of the concert, one of the students practically yelled out to everyone present: there was his uncle in the orchestra. How special to see and hear someone to whom you were related—a successful Roma musician. It was clear the other students could identify with pride as well. I couldn't have been more pleased.

AFTERWORD:
THE NEXT CHAPTERS

Peace Corps led the way. Without the opportunity to be a Volunteer, the direction of my life would have been vastly different. I was already curious about people whose lives were different than mine, but my many experiences in the Philippines took me out of my comfort zone. I didn't know how I would fare ahead of time, but I was willing to try to connect, unafraid of the consequences.

Meeting Nate, a former Peace Corps Volunteer in Thailand, basically charted my future with him and my subsequent paths in life. He was positive, upbeat, and enthusiastic about the same things I loved. He essentially wanted what I wanted out of life, even though our backgrounds couldn't have been more different. Our primary connector was an emphasis on education and the Peace Corps experience itself. After we met and married, he led the way through work he found in Asia, Africa, and Europe. I was never just a follower but intensely involved in the life we chose for ourselves. Then, before we left our peripatetic life behind, I had to think about what I wanted to do with the rest of it in the US.

While we still lived abroad, I completed several cross-cultural workshops at the Summer Intercultural Communication Institute, based in Portland, OR, to better grasp the whole process of understanding another culture. As a result, I was able to lead workshops for others. Then, with my interest in people, culture, and the arts, museums seemed an interesting next step.

In Salem, MA, I worked initially for The House of the

Seven Gables, directing education and researching African American history in the city. Later, I joined the Peabody Essex Museum, where I helped develop their first African gallery and created programs around it that attempted to include African Americans in the area. Later, back in Maine, I managed the Joshua Chamberlain House Museum and learned about the Civil War from the docents. In these instances, my nearly seven years in Ghana, West Africa, gradually deepened my interest in African American history, their struggles, and lives. Next, I applied to teach at Midcoast Senior College based in Brunswick, Maine, at a friend's suggestion. After acceptance, I researched for at least six months before I felt confident to talk with some knowledge on everything from the Atlantic Slave Trade, to racism, white privilege, reparations, and Critical Race Theory, as examples. After ten courses and eight years, I have grown more confident as I have moved forward on this track.

Yet, there is still so much to learn and to teach white Americans.

During the same time, I participated in a writing group for several years, where I tried my hand at capturing and sharing my life in various countries. Since we read our work aloud, I could gauge some interest in what I had to say. What I didn't get was technical help in writing. So, when I eventually decided to try to write a book, I was more unprepared than I thought I would be. Nancy, my editor and publisher, was incredibly helpful in this regard.

So, what did I learn about myself from living in five countries for nearly sixteen years? I learned that I was okay with living a relatively unsettled life. I enjoyed the unpredictability of where we would end up next, despite the enormous work of eventually moving a family. I found the prospects of the next adventure—whatever and wherever it might be—exciting. I could be flexible.

I learned I would always be "the other" wherever we lived and worked. I was an *orang puteh* in Malaysia, an obroni in Ghana, both instances referring to me as a white person. I stood out in every country except Macedonia, where most people were white. Sometimes it was with mistaken adoration for Americans. Sometimes it was with scorn for the Americans. But it was impossible to ignore. Even though we were not wealthy by American standards, we were usually financially better off than most host country nationals. We had more, so we shared. I also tried to respond to that inequality with respect and personal interest. That may not have completely immersed me in the culture, but I believe it helped, even though sometimes I made mistakes. I learned that there were lots of connections among several cultures.

The Mangyan script related to Indian Sanskrit, echoing a distant history. Over centuries, the Chinese had left their artifacts in the Philippines, like the honey jar trade item the Mangyans gave me. The Spaniards left their traditions and fashion ideas to the people of the Philippines. In Indonesia, the wayang kulit puppet shows came directly from the Indian Ramayana story. To my surprise, I detected brightly colored Indonesian designs in the commercial cloth known as "African Cloth" in Ghana, owing to the earlier colonial presence of the Dutch in both spheres of influence. I was amazed to learn the significance of the calves of men's legs to the creation story among the Mangyans and the ethnic Karens of Northern Thailand. The Ottomans left their recipes, baths, and stables for modern Macedonians to recreate. These were just a few of the connections I discovered. I learned about the many dissimilarities between cultures as well.

While I know people everywhere all have the same needs for shelter, warmth, water, food, and good health, they create ways to take care of those aspects differently. I had difficulty eating with my hands in Asia and Africa, but it was common in both areas. In several countries, it was not unusual to see men in sarongs or other fabric tied around their waists instead of pants. When we showed people photos of our Maine house of wood, they laughed at our risk for the possibility of fire, and concrete was more common everywhere (except for bamboo or mud houses in rural areas.) Many in Asia couldn't tolerate milk from cows, while we considered it a staple in the US. Asians and Africans tended to prefer a more spicy diet than Americans, perhaps because it had historically kept food fresher in a tropical climate. Textiles could speak a language in some cultures, like the Asante of Ghana, before writing was created there. Desserts were practically unknown in Ghana, apart from an occasional sweet available as street fare. The irony, of course, was that their ancestors were taken to Brazil and the West Indies as enslaved people to work on sugar plantations, which pleased the palates of Europeans and filled their pockets with fortunes. As Americans, we still live with a taste for sugar.

In this book, recalling the names of peoples and places, particular foods, and textiles helped me tell stories. I painted with a few broad brushstrokes in words, all things that were dear, rare, or delicious to me—fascinating food that I still long for, specific events, and places that I don't want to forget. Above all, I enjoyed documenting the names of individuals I will always cherish, wonderful friends I still love, even if I never see them again. Everything I learned and experienced while living and traveling overseas has been a major factor in shaping me into the person I am today. I can't imagine my life without these opportunities. They have immeasurably enriched me. I see my life in these countries as part of an enormous gain, never a loss, to my life today. The journeys became my life. For all of this, I am grateful.

SPECIAL STORIES
AND
SUGGESTIONS

The author working on a fiber wall piece for a show in Maine, 1975.

NIGHTMARES ABOUT POISONOUS SNAKES

Before moving to a tropical location where we were to spend two to seven years, I experienced frequent nightmares about snakes. As it turned out, all of our destination countries had poisonous snakes: the Philippines, Malaysia, Sri Lanka, Ghana, and Macedonia. I was deathly afraid of snakes, yet managed to live happily in each place, once I arrived. Still, the fear did not abate over time. In each country I had at least one near encounter with a poisonous snake.

I actually encountered my first poisonous snake back in a little town in Kansas when I was five years old. We were at my grandmother's home where all my relatives gathered to enjoy some summertime picnicking on the lawn. The house sat in a huge lot with a big fenced in yard which included my grandmother's enormous garden. I had gone into the house for something, and when I came out, I stepped over a rattlesnake lying under the lip of the threshold. It was lying quietly, perhaps hoping to be unseen, but I saw it and ran to tell the family. Nobody believed me at first, saying it was probably just some loose piece of insulation under the door. Finally, my uncle came to look, and, sure enough, I was right. I don't remember what happened next, but he killed the snake.

There were no more snake encounters until I went overseas. We lived in a very urban area in Kansas so that was not surprising. The same was true of most of my time in the Philippines. But the summer I went to live with the Mangyans on the island mountains of Oriental Mindoro, I had a close encounter. I climbed from the lowland town of Mansalay, next to the sea, for more than two hours up a mountain. After an hour in the high heat and humidity, I had to rest on a log. It was only after I got up that I saw out of the corner of my eye, a cobra slipped away from beside the log, leaving its skin behind. The cobra had just shed while I was resting above it. Despite this scare, I kept walking on to the village of Panatayan, where I worked most of the summer. I never saw another snake while I lived there.

When Nate and I next lived in Malaysia, our home was in a development of small identical concrete houses. One day I saw a clutch of newly hatched cobras in the drainage ditch outside the house. I asked my Malay neighbor about them. He suggested not to fool with them, as they were just as lethal as their parents. Some months later our dog started barking her head off in the driveway. From the living room, with just the metal folding screen between me and the outdoors, I went to see what was going on. As soon as I saw the cobra heading toward our living room, I quickly closed the wooden doors to the outside, and ran out through the carport to alert some Malays working on the road. I yelled "*Ular, Ular,*" and the workmen came running. Their intent was to kill the snake, but first they teased it as I watched safely from inside the house. Then they slaughtered it with a machete. I wasn't prepared to see that.

I had another close encounter with a cobra while in Malaysia. I began to take batik lessons with an artist. He lived in a *kampong* some distance from the road. I had to walk a long path, in a field of high weeds, to his house. Once, a cobra crossed my path just a foot in front of me. I didn't know if it was aware of me, but I walked carefully and slowly on the path after that. Meanwhile, we often saw snakes on the beach and swimming in the South China Sea. They were definitely everywhere.

In Sri Lanka, we lived with our two children, ages seven and twelve, in Cinnamon Gardens, fairly far from the middle of Colombo. Our house had a nice front lawn but backed up next to a big concrete sewage ditch. Because we had air conditioning, we kept the windows and doors shut to maintain the coolness inside. But one night I got up to go to the bathroom and there was a small snake in the hallway. I knew it was not a cobra, but there were lots of smaller snakes that could be poisonous. As the snake backtracked around the corner under a chest, I woke up Nate. He went downstairs to get a knife from the kitchen. Meanwhile, I had to sit on the stairs, watching the snake's possible moves so I could inform Nate. He was able to kill it and put it in a jar to take to the nurse at the American Embassy for identification. It turned out not to be poisonous, but we had to figure out how it got in. We found that a closet in the upstairs hall had open slats instead of a closed window, that led onto the roof. That was the only possible entry. We boarded the area up the next day.

We found that snakes could climb trellises while living in Ghana. There, on the second floor of our Cape Coast house, we had an enormous balcony. The balcony was a wonderful place to be in the daytime, to get some sun and enjoy the view, or in the early evening to catch a little breeze and gather for an outdoor supper before the mosquitoes descended. One day, while Nate

Green venomous viper traveling across our balcony in Cape Coast, Ghana, 1994.

was in a lawn chair reading, he discovered a yellow-green snake slithering across the balcony. Alarmed—because he knew it was a poisonous viper—he threw a shoe at it until it went back down the trellis.

There were even more alarming issues with cobras in Ghana. Nate and I often had to go to Accra on business, and occasionally left our fourteen-year-old son, Sean, at home with Evans, who worked for us. One day, two of them walked through the small unused garage, a cobra rose up out of a paint can and spit at Evans. Sean was scared. He consulted our book on spitting cobras and learned that their spit could destroy the skin on a person's hand. There were photos to prove it. Fortunately, Evans and his hand turned out to be fine.

A few months later, Nate and I were in Accra again, while a huge rainstorm raged in Cape Coast. When we got home that night, we approached a wheelbarrow on the patio, full of two dead ten-foot black king cobras. John, the caretaker, and Evans had killed the cobra pair as they slipped across our flooded patio. The hard rain had apparently filled their hole in the yard and pushed them out. I was terrified to see this but very grateful that nothing had happened to Sean or anyone else.

After that we didn't see any snakes around the house, but we often saw them crossing the highway. One day we even stopped to see a huge python beside the road—a crowd of villagers appeared to be bewitched by this enormous, but relatively harmless snake. It could eat small animals, but only a small unattended child was ever in danger. This one was easily thirty feet long.

Later, when we moved to Accra, one side of our house backed up against the jungle. When Yemi, my colleague and our soon-to-be roommate, showed us the house, I asked if he had ever seen cobras in the area. Perhaps sensing my fear, Yemi assured me that he hadn't. Just then a cobra zig-zagged across the driveway below us. Yemi looked at me then as if I had conjured up the snake. I returned his look with a wary smile. He later put stout sticks at all entrances to the house so that we could beat off any cobras that came around. I never saw another one in Accra.

When we lived in Macedonia, I never saw any snakes. I understood that poisonous snakes existed there, but they escaped our notice. We lived in the large capital city of Skopje, which might have explained their absence. I was happy to be finished with snakes, poisonous or otherwise.

LEARNING TO TALK

Learning new languages was not my strength. English, my first language, was my strength. And, yet, when the prospect of living in other countries presented itself, I knew it was important to learn the language the best I could. While I found it tedious, I soon realized that language could often symbolically represent a culture. Just like artifacts, particular words in a language told a lot about a place and a people. For instance, some languages didn't have words for snow and ice, because there wasn't any. And some had no word for art, even though the culture, like that of Bali, was full of art. Determined to forge ahead, despite my relative inability to become fluent, I did my best.

Tagalog was the first language I learned in Hawaii Peace Corps training, en route to the Philippines. Talking in Tagalog with Jose for a couple of hours in the morning and a couple of hours in the afternoon was very draining. We sat in the old school rooms in big groups, repeating, repeating and repeating—for three months. I couldn't wait to get outside in the sun, walk through the countryside, meet the neighbors, socialize. Anything but feeling forced into another language. But in the end it was so appreciated when I tried to speak Tagalog in my barrio of San Juan, Malolos. Also, so many Spanish words flowed through Tagalog, I recognized half of them much later in life, when my daughter-in-law spoke in fluent Spanish. And, Tagalog had a smattering of English thrown in. Languages began to tell me a lot about the history of a place.

In the short time I spent among the Mangyan people, I learned some of their language while teaching them Tagalog. What I learned of Mangyan was taught casually, mostly in conversation with Wili, on the floor of her nipa hut. I learned through a combination of sign language, drawings and written words. First, I discovered that Mangyans could recognize any written words upside down, sideways, or right side up. I thought that most unusual, but fascinating. They were looking at the visual patterns. The Mangyans loved writing their own poetry, called *ambahans*, carved onto pieces of bamboo as gifts. I thought this was very touching and lovely.

I noticed, much later, traveling through India that many characters in Mangyan looked like Sanskrit. I was amazed, but later learned about the influence of India in Indonesia. Their written language must have accompanied the people who eventually drifted across the sea from Borneo to parts of the Philippines. Unlike Tagalog, Mangyan did not reflect either English or Spanish. Avoiding the colonizers in the lowlands, the Mangyans had kept to the mountains for centuries, and held onto their culture and language.

We learned Malay with another couple in the Peace Corps Office in DC. We were all headed to new posts in Malaysia. I don't remember the name of the teacher, but I enjoyed being with just two other people. And, when we got to Malaysia, there were lots of opportunities to speak in our small town of Kuantan on the east coast. Of course, as in the Philippines, Malaysia's background included colonialism by English speakers. The main difference was that they came from England, not the United States.

The other interesting fact was that Malay was akin to Bahasa Indonesia, the Indonesian language. So, you could speak Malay in both places and be understood. But Bahasa always seemed more sophisticated to me. That speaks to the history too: India established more than one Hindu-Buddhist kingdom among the Islands of the East Indies (Indonesia) between the sixth and the sixteenth centuries. Since India was already composed of several highly developed cultures, it stands to reason that the language would reflect that. Still, I understood that Malay came first.

Upon settling into Sri Lanka, we tried to learn Sinhala, the language of the dominant group in the country, the Singhalese, who had arrived on this island around the sixth century BC. This time we learned as a family in our home. After the kids returned from school a couple of times a week, our language tutor came over and we all sat around the dining room table, attempting to learn and speak. It was a great experience because we were all trying together—ages seven, twelve, thirty-nine, and forty-one. Later, following a school field trip down the coast, Windi reported that she was able to speak to the fishermen and they understood her. She was very proud, especially since it seemed to impress the other kids in her class.

While Sri Lanka went through several name changes under three major powers—Portuguese, Dutch, and English—I don't remember detecting their influence on the language. Of course, not being fluent, I could have been wrong. The language was very old, coming with people out of northern India to this island nation, along with Buddhism, for which Sri Lanka became known. Their written language was old too, slightly resembling Sanskrit, but unique in its own way. It's characters created lovely shapes as they seemed to artistically prance across a page.

Finally, we left Asia and in a few years headed to our next post in Ghana. In Africa the languages were not even vaguely related to those in Asia. This time Nate and I sat on our balcony with our son, Sean, and dug into Fanti with our new language teacher. Fanti was among the group of Akan languages spoken by the Akan people who arrived over time into this area migrating from the Northwest Sahara Desert. The Akans, descendants of the ancient Ghana Empire, were all over central and coastal Ghana, and they each had their own language variations, but they were related. The Fantis were on the coast, where we lived at the time. They had been the middlemen in the Atlantic Slave Trade, between the Asantes who spoke *twi* and grew wealthy, and the foreigners, who grew even more wealthy. Before colonial times, there was no written language, because the culture was oral. That all changed when the Akans became part of Britain's Gold Coast colony. That also explained why there were different spellings for many Akan words. For example, Asante was also spelled Ashanti, both names referring to the same people.

In earlier times, Akan meaning and symbolism were expressed

through the arts, within textile designs and proverbs. The cultures of the Akan were very rich and interesting. Although as engaged as we could be with the culture, unfortunately, we never became fluent in Fanti, despite living in Ghana for nearly seven years total.

The author with her favorite language teacher and friend, Jasmine, together in Skopje, Macedonia, 2006, while learning Macedonian by journeying through Skopje to visit museums, markets, coffee shops, super markets, etc.

I blame that on the fact that schools and government all used English as the first language. But, it probably also meant we didn't try as hard as we might have.

Macedonian was the apex of language learning for me. While Nate took lessons with a woman in his office, I ventured out and interviewed language instructors. I posted my cell phone number in the Peace Corps office in Skopje and soon had three prospects. The language teacher I chose—Jasmine—seemed most enthusiastic about what I wanted to do. I was thrilled. I told her I wanted to learn the language by walking around the city, focusing on its different features—shops, museums, galleries, markets, and restaurants. She agreed and off we went, meeting two or three times a week. Macedonian was difficult, a Slavic language, and few people spoke English. Whatever Jasmine and I did, we always ended up in a café at the end of the lesson. Cafes were everywhere: along the big Vardar river, tucked in city alleyways, in new malls, in fancy western European restaurants that offered large lattes and cappuccinos, as well as within the walls of ancient Csarija. I loved being in Csarija, inside a courtyard surrounded by the structures that the Ottomans had built during their hundreds of years of occupation. These courtyards, former stables and inns, now restaurants and coffee shops, were decorated in beautiful trees and flowers. I felt I was really entering old Macedonia. When we had coffee, it was always espresso in small cups.

It was ironic that in the country where I spent the least amount of time that I probably learned the most. I think this was due to having years of experience, knowing what I wanted in a language, and, finally, how I wanted to get it. The other aspect that became so important to me was that Jasmine and I became fast friends. Sometimes she would confide in me and ask my advice. She also got married while we were there, and Nate and I witnessed their very interesting wedding, Macedonian style. It involved the town hall, plus the Macedonian Orthodox Church, where bread was broken and crowns bestowed. The reception that followed in a hotel, offered delicious Macedonian delicacies, lively music for dancing, and, of course, espresso coffee.

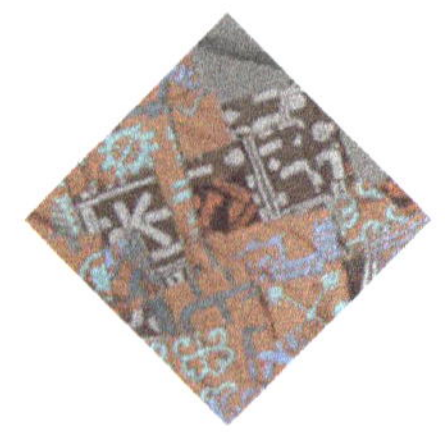

THOSE WHO WORKED FOR US

Expatriates who lived in developing countries, as we did, usually had servants. We had people working for us, and though we never called them servants, I suppose it was only a matter of semantics. We had been spoiled in the US with electric washing machines, dryers, dishwashers, vacuum cleaners, etc. In many of the five countries we lived in, I wouldn't have had a clue—nor would I have wanted to spend the time—washing clothes in buckets outside, scrubbing them with stones, laying them on bushes to dry, ironing underwear, sheets and towels (because of harmful insect larva), then navigating the open air town market for the best buys. In the beginning I loved poking around in the markets, enjoyed viewing beautiful exotic (to me) fruits and vegetables, as well as unrecognizable meats, but I couldn't get the best prices because I was a white foreigner. It was better if I went with a local person. Having assistance with cooking and cleaning meant that I could do other things—things of more interest to me, things I was more capable of doing. Things I hoped made a difference in the world. Having someone to cook and clean was special, addicting, and a privilege I tried not to see as an entitlement. And for the people working for us, the job paid very well because, as Americans, we were comparatively well off. Expatriates weren't the only ones who had help though, most local families did too. They probably paid less, and often hired their nieces or nephews from the village, who were only given food and shelter.

But one of the things that many people overlooked was how wonderful it was that this person you had hired was perhaps the first individual in the culture that you got to know. They could help you understand things, you could ask them questions—assuming your languages matched even a little— and observe, learning what it was, essentially, to be a Filipino, Malaysian, Sri Lankan, Ghanaian or Macedonian.

The first helper I knew as a Peace Corps Volunteer, was Manung in Malolos, Bulacan, the Philippines. She was an older woman, but I admired the fact that she could take care of a family of six, plus me. After breakfast, she began the washing and cleaning for the day, then made dinner for everyone. Manung discovered early on that what I loved most for breakfast was the bread called *pan de sal* (salt bread literally). She would go to the market before I got up and buy it for me, still hot, and delicious. When I came home from teaching in the afternoons, she would just be picking up the clothes off the grass, the bushes, and the fence, ready to iron before dinner. She was an amazing woman, and every time I visited my family in the Philippines, she was there. I always gave her a great hug.

Malaysia was different, as Nate and I were on our own together in Kuantan. There was already a woman working in our house when we came, but she decided to leave. She was Chinese, and her previous employer was also Chinese, so I think that was important to her. I am not sure how I found Josephine, but she was warm and caring. Indian Malaysian, she lived in an area of Kuantan that was entirely Indian, separate from the Chinese in town, and most of the Malays around the edge of Kuantan, or in the smaller villages. She didn't cook for us, but she had a lovely personality. Two years later when I brought our newborn daughter home from the hospital, she reached out to hold her. She asked for the remains of Windi's umbilical cord, which she enclosed in a locket and gave to me for Windi when she was older. It was for Windi's good fortune. And when Nate was away and I was alone, Josephine would come spend the night in the house.

Later, we moved to Kuala Lumpur for a year, just as another American couple were departing Malaysia. So, we asked if Chin would like to work for us. Chin was a force of nature, so enthusiastic about everything, never complaining, always willing. I had to be careful not to take advantage of her, she had such a positive attitude about everything. And she cooked, so we enjoyed lots of delicious

Chinese meals, plus she would babysit Windi when I went out. I only went out when Windi was napping or asleep at night, because I felt guilty otherwise.

By the time Sri Lanka was our destination, Windi was already twelve, and now we had Sean too, age seven. So, it was a family adventure in South Asia, having left Southeast Asia behind. The whole culture was different, from the look of people, to food, to clothes, to homes, nearly everything. When a woman named Rita appeared at my door in Colombo, asking for work as a cook, I was impressed. She could speak and read good English, cook dishes from recipe books, and had a lot of experience in the neighborhood. I didn't even bother to ask for recommendations. She must have been with us, happily, for two years before Nate started thinking money was missing from his wallet upstairs. It was happening on a Saturday while he and Windi were taking guitar lessons in the living room downstairs. One day we visited Rita, her husband and young daughter in their modest home. From the living room I could see that the room behind held boxes from floor to ceiling, and in one of them a sash from one of Windi's dresses was hanging out. It was then we knew that she had been stealing from us. We confronted her, and with tears on both sides, we asked her to go.

Meanwhile, Mrs. Fernando was taking care of our family in all the other ways, cleaning, washing and ironing (this time with machines from the American Embassy.) She was a wonderful older woman who came on the train from a village some thirty kilometers south of us. She always arrived in a beautiful saree, worked in a simple house dress, then changed back again into her saree for the train ride home. She was a proud woman whom I appreciated greatly. She stayed with us until the end of our three years in Sri Lanka and we kept connected by letters for a long time afterward.

Since I was by now working as an admissions counselor in the Colombo Children's School, in Rita's place we hired another older woman to cook, whom we called Mrs. M. She was delightfully game, and though she hadn't much experience working for foreigners, she was willing to give it a go. We tried to alternate dinners between American and Sri Lankan. Once I asked if she would make a quiche and I showed her how to make a crust in my *Joy of Cooking* cookbook. I thought the drawings would do the trick. You can imagine how amazed I was when she showed me the beautifully woven dough strips sinking into the wet, milky quiche. I realized I had shown her a drawing to top a typical pie crust, not a quiche. So we all had a good laugh about it and, in the end the quiche was delicious, despite some damp strips of crust.

By the time we arrived in Cape Coast, Ghana, Windi was in college and Sean was with us, a young teenager. We first hired Angie to cook. She was young but had married an older German expatriate man, quite wealthy. She admitted to me that she had been unfaithful and became pregnant with a young Ghanaian boyfriend. When Angie's German husband died, he left her his Mercedes Benz. Angie's boyfriend stole the car, sold it in Accra, and flew off to Europe. Angie completely fell apart. I liked her and thought asking her to work for us might help. It did, and we grew to love her and her daughter, Susie. With Angie, we started the tradition of the three A's: alternating American, Asian and African food for dinner. It represented where we had lived overseas, and was a great model for meal planning that was exciting and different every night.

We also hired a young man named, Evans, from a nearby village. He was introduced by a cousin in Cape Coast. We liked him and asked him to take care of the house. Unfortunately, he and Angie didn't get along at all. I think Angie saw him as an unsophisticated villager, which in a way he was at the time. So there was a lot of screaming and yelling between Angie and Evans. Angie eventually left to start her own business, selling food on the street. She was still in town, so we saw her every once in a while. But Evans continued to work for us until we left Cape Coast. For a long time he did everything. I showed him how to cook several dishes, and like most Ghanaians, he could both speak and read English. He would often make dinner in the afternoon and refrigerate it for us, which was a terrific boon. After his work day was over, I would take it out and warm it up in the evening. I liked Evans very much, but found it a little disconcerting when I discovered that, before he emptied our waste baskets he would sit down and read everything we threw away:

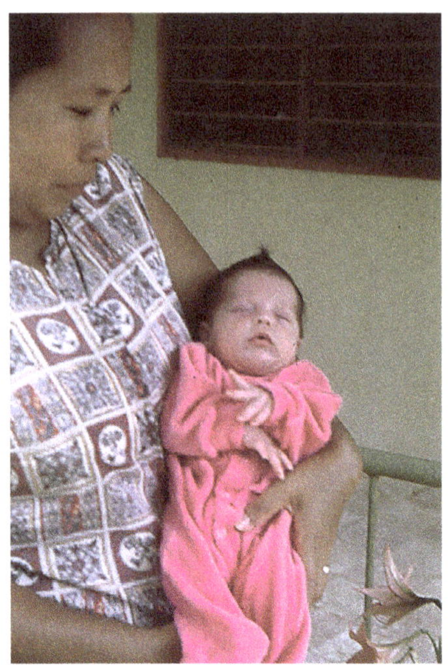

Josephine holding our newborn baby, Windi, in Malaysia, 1971. Josephine was delightful, worked for us in Kuantan, and adored Windi.

Mrs. Fernando, a lovely person, and our housekeeper in Colombo, Sri Lanka, 1983-86.

Angie, our animated cook in Cape Coast, Ghana, but who didn't get along with Evans, who also worked for us, 1991.

Evans, our terrific housekeeper (right) in Cape Coast, Ghana, and John, the landlord's caretaker (left), about 1994.

Kind Martha, with her daughter, who cooked for us in Cape Coast, Ghana after Angie left, and later in Accra, when I co-directed the SIT African Arts and Culture semester abroad program, 1995.

Aiysha, the gentle young woman who helped me in my rented house in Accra, Ghana, when I worked for the American Ambassador, 1993.

personal letters, bank statements, advertisements, etc. We had to be careful and started tearing things up before getting rid of them.

One day we decided to check out the old, downtrodden, former British colonial tennis club where Nate wanted to play. There was a woman there who cooked and sold kebabs to those who came to enjoy tennis, along with Club Beer. Martha was very laid back and friendly. We started talking and eventually she came to cook for us, freeing up Evans, and replacing Angie. She was such a kind young woman, we became very attached. She was divorced, but had a couple of young kids in school. Later, following our departure from Cape Coast for a few months in the US, on our return to live in Accra while I was running a college semester abroad program, Martha joined us again to cook.

In the year before that, I began renting a small house in Accra, in order to work part time for the American Ambassador. Nate came to Accra on weekends, or I went back to Cape Coast. But I inherited an amazing young woman named Aiysha who did everything for me. She was gentle and kind and smart as a whip. I enjoyed her company, especially since I was alone most of the time, and she stayed with me. She would cook up some cream of wheat for my breakfast every morning (I had access to the American commissary at that time) and enclosed it in a plastic container, which I would lay on my office air conditioner to eat when I was hungry. She would also make whatever I wanted for a simple dinner.

Our last overseas assignment was for a year in Skopje, Macedonia. The apartment we rented came with a woman, Fatima, who kept it up. We didn't hire her, but the apartment owner did, probably to keep track of his renters, which was not a bad idea. We cooked for ourselves (there was a dishwasher) or ate out in the many great restaurants nearby. We asked the owner for covers to protect the leather sofas in the living room from our cat, even though the covers looked rather old fashioned. Even more old fashioned were all of the tatted doilies from the tables and armrests, which I removed. Fatima kept putting them back, because that was where they belonged. We could barely understand each other, except through body language. Plus, Fatima, was also a Roma speaking Romani. Despite our language barrier, she was wonderful, listening to her radio every day as she worked, loud pop music blasting in the background. And we smiled at each other as we passed in the hall. I wished I had gotten to know her better. Working with the Roma students at the Sumnal center was the closest I came to understanding her life.

THE CROSS-CULTURAL
WOMEN'S GROUPS

I looked around my Kuala Lumpur dining room at the women I had invited for lunch: a British woman, a Canadian, a German, and a wonderful Malaysian batik artist of Indian descent named Grace Selvanayagam. I was quite happy to have such a wonderfully diverse group together. Lunch was going to be a casserole made from apples and cheese, expensive in KL, but hopefully not controversial, very American. This was Malaysia in 1970, and the lunch was my first attempt at what later grew into a template for cross-cultural women's groups in all future overseas assignments.

The next country I lived in was Sri Lanka, beginning in 1983. As soon as I met Indira, who became my good friend, she suggested we form a cross-cultural women's group. I wasn't sure exactly what she had in mind, but I was game. She invited some Sri Lankan women, and I invited some expatriates I had met. We both encouraged each woman to invite someone else from another country. In the end we had Thai, English, Mexican, and Dutch, American and Sri Lankan women, if I remember correctly. Our first meeting was at my house, to decide what direction to take this group.

Our time together in Colombo was often almost magical as we became friends and learned about Sri Lanka at the same time. I remember going to a movie by a Sinhalese screen writer. Once we were visited by a Buddhist nun, a white woman who had become a Buddhist, in a country that was founded on Buddhism. We looked at sapphires with Siri, for which Sri Lanka was famous, and they were beautiful. We tried on sarees to understand how

221

very complicated they were to put on and wear. Watching nine yards of cloth being folded and wrapped to make a woman look beautiful, was very enlightening. We read books and went to plays by Sri Lankan artists and playwrights. My favorite performance was the premiere of the Sanaa Ballet. It was exquisite, and made me feel so very glad that I was living in Sri Lanka.

When we arrived in Cape Coast, Ghana in 1990, there were almost no expatriates living there. It seemed odd since historically this had been the British capital of the Gold Coast, not to mention an earlier place of slave trading. Many Europeans had lived and moved through here over more than four hundred years, including the Portuguese, the Dutch, the Swedes and the British. But, when I wanted to start a cross-cultural group, as far as I knew there was only the Dutch woman from the restaurant/hotel up the coast. She was invited, of course, and several Ghanaian women I knew agreed to join. The problem for me was that most didn't really want to explore cross-culturally. They wanted to join hands to raise money for the poor. Certainly a worthwhile endeavor, it just wasn't what I had in mind. So, my idea fell apart.

When I found work in Accra, things changed dramatically. I invited the Minister of Culture, a woman; I invited Marian,

A meeting of the cross-cultural women's group in Colombo, Sri Lanka, with author second from right, and best Sri Lankan friend, Indira, third from right, 1985.

Edmund's wife; and Jackie, the Peace Corps director's wife. I invited several women I had met at the American Embassy and many were interested to join, including the Ambassador's wife, Bonnie. Her interest gave the cross-cultural women's group a sort of social cache. It had become a good group to join, and several Ghanaian women did. I couldn't have been happier.

As before, my goal was that the Ghanaian and the expatriate women create opportunities to get to know each other better, by exploring Ghanaian cultures. We shared our individual country's foods, we learned about African trade beads, and met with three weavers, representing the Asante and the Ewe cultures. But the most exciting get-together was when someone organized the meeting of three Queen Mothers. A Queen Mother had a very important role to play in Asante culture. So, to be able to meet three Queen Mothers at once, dressed in their best cloths and regalia, was a thrilling opportunity. Despite the fact that I had wanted this group to continue as a small cross-cultural group, word got out and nearly one hundred women showed up for this eye-opening occasion.

When I arrived in Skopje, Macedonia in 2006 the situation was entirely different. Malaysia, Sri Lanka, and Ghana had all been colonized by the old British Empire, but not Macedonia. In Macedonia, a former Yugoslav state, almost no one spoke English unless they worked for a British or United States agency, the UN, or studied abroad. In order to start a cross-cultural women's group I went to the International Women's Association. They met in a restaurant, and during lunch you could sign up for any side group that interested you. So I put a sign-up sheet on the bulletin board and waited. At the end of lunch I was delighted to find that seven women had signed up, from different countries: Italy, Great Britain, Turkey, Greece, Armenia and Canada, plus two Americans.

The first meeting took place at my apartment. I explained that I was interested in learning about Macedonian culture while getting to know both expatriate and Macedonian women. I asked them to ask at least one Macedonian friend to join us. There was a pregnant pause, then one woman spoke up: "I guess none of us know any." I was rather shocked. So I set out the next day to see who I could find among the Macedonians I had met. I invited Danica, my next door neighbor first. Then I invited Mine, the wife of my husband's colleague. And I invited the woman doctor who had seen me when I had some breathing problems. They all agreed. I also asked them to invite any other Macedonian women who might enjoy this group.

The turnout was good and we had some fabulous experiences. Someone got us into a rehearsal of the National Ballet, where we got to check out costumes and talk with a few ballerinas, as well as watch them dance. Another person said she could get us in to see the National Folk Dance Company, and that was a very special performance. We watched an amazing movie together, created by a Macedonian, which challenged our idea of time. We attended a jazz performance in Carsija, the old marketplace. We were guided through a museum of traditional Macedonian antique costumes. My favorite afternoon was with a Macedonian archaeologist who had discovered and unearthed an ancient flute, which he both lectured about, and played for the first time in centuries. We were all captivated.

At the end of every meeting of the cross-cultural women's group, we had coffee together at some café. This coffee tradition was very strong in Macedonia, and in good weather, which was much of the year, most restaurants offered a place to sit outside. It was a trend that has been taken up, finally, by many American restaurants.

The first meeting of the Cross-cultural Women's Group in Skopje, Macedonia met at my apartment, 2006.

GETTING TO KNOW
A PLACE AND ITS PEOPLE

Other than a few sessions in cross-cultural training before going to live in the Philippines, I didn't yet have a handle on how to enter and interact in a culture successfully. Experience helped, but mistakes were made. It was only after returning from Sri Lanka that I decided to take some workshops to better help me accommodate myself to the next culture. Luckily I found the Intercultural Communication Institute in Portland, Oregon. It offered many interesting and useful workshops during the summer. Here is what I learned, both from them and from my own personal experience. Most of the suggestions are for those spending a significant amount of time in a particular culture or country. But many can be used on any visit of at least a week, as well.

After a week of settling in:

Start to **spiral out** from where you are—whether it is from a hostel, a hotel, a friend's house, or your rental apartment/house.

Try to **meet your neighbors** next door even if you don't know the language yet. But learn the basics: words for greetings, introducing yourself, and thank you. Most of the rest you can accomplish with a smile and body language.

Go to the **shops down the street or around the corner**. Greet the shopkeeper, point to things of interest, and generally get an idea of what is available. Buy something small if you can. Don't forget to thank him or her afterwards.

Go for **lunch at the nearest restaurant**. Ask for a menu and for the ingredients of some of the dishes. Sometimes there are photos for foreigners. Better yet, just order something without knowing what it is. The waiter and the manager will want to help you in order to be sure you return.

Venture out **a little farther each day,** enlarging the spiral. Find out where the nearest coffee house, bar, library, school, church, museum, and government tourism office is in town. For a smaller village, there may be fewer of these destinations, but there will be something you can find out about and discover. Introduce yourself and your country wherever you go, as well as why you are here, even if you have to mime some of it. Better still, learn how to say why you are in their country and what you are doing, in the local language. That way people will begin to understand your origins and your reason for being here.

During the next couple of weeks:

Find out where you can hire a **language instructor**. Check around at work, at the Embassy, or, if there is a Peace Corps office, they will know. That person will not only help you navigate the language, but may also show you around, if you ask.

An **Interpreter** can also do the job, but is likely to spend less time teaching you the language, rather translating it instead.

Try finding a **guide**, if you want someone mainly to show you around the city, town, village or countryside. Ask that person to also introduce you to people he or she knows along the way. Or ask to be introduced to particular persons in their respective roles.

Sometimes all you need is an **informant** to guide you to places you can go on your own. It can be someone you met on the plane, a friend, or a business associate. These people are likely to give you "sound bites" of a specific nature.

Occasionally, you will find a **mentor,** a local teacher, a minister, or missionary, who can help you with language and culture, as well as introduce you to people and places. This will likely be someone you will want to spend some significant time with.

After a month:

By now **you have probably met several persons** from both the local culture and perhaps some expatriates as well. This is the ideal time, if you are interested, to see how many might be willing to form a cross-cultural men's or women's group to get to know one another better. Winning can happen on both sides.

Find a focus for your group. It should be a theme that all cultural participants will enjoy. Also, it should be something that one or more host country nationals (local persons) can show the rest of you from elsewhere. In my experience, choosing the broad theme of the arts was very interesting and enriching for the cross-cultural women's groups that I started. Together we visited dance companies behind the scenes, met local authors, went to temples and historic sites, lectures at universities, concerts, plays and movies. Other groups might want to visit architecture, ancient ruins, fishing, hiking, churches, the opera, restaurants or bars, to name a few ideas.

The point of the cross-cultural groups is to **get to know local people,** and to help them get to know you as expatriates, through some medium that both will find interesting and enjoyable.

Use all of your senses in the process:

Listen to the language, its intonation, whether it is a tonal language, and the style in which people talk.

Look at the speaker's eyes, their facial expressions, their hands, their body language. Do they like touching you, want to be close and feel your breath, look down shyly, or gesticulate boldly with their hands? Look at books about the culture both before and after encounters with local people and learn what you can.

Taste all food offered, if at all possible. If clean water is likely to be a problem, kindly defer and ask for a bottled drink or just don't having anything to drink. Try different meals in restaurants and keep track of what you like. Also try food in outdoor markets as sometimes the stall keeper will offer you a taste of something obviously new to you. Always thank them, and buy the item, if you like it.

Take the opportunity to **touch** things that are remarkable in the country/culture (with permission, if appropriate)—their hand woven textiles, wooden carvings, the sand on the beach, old cobblestones on ancient streets, etc. Using your tactile sense is another way of enjoying a new place.

Take the time to **smell** rich coffee brewing, the aroma of new bread baking, the fragrance of a curry, or that of flowers you walk by.

D.I.E. method

If you have a problem understanding something, Use the D.I.E. method*:

D stands for describe. It means it is important to try to objectively describe a situation, food or person, before judging them. It is hard to do, and most of us just leap to judgment. But in another culture, this is not a solution to understanding what is happening and why.

I stands for interpret. Often you can't do this by yourself. So, ask someone standing next to you. If you still don't understand, just mimic what others are doing around you. Finally, just stand silently, or nod in respect. If necessary, quietly walk away after signifying with your eyes or a nod, a little respect. If you still can't figure it out, when you see your language instructor, ask them the meaning of the event. Try to make amends if that seems appropriate.

E stands for evaluate. If you have described and tried to interpret, then you are free to evaluate or judge. Sometimes your evaluation need only be to yourself. If you want to get along, it is usually best to not offend. Sometimes, however, it is important to defer because of your values. Be sure you figure out what personal values you can't cross, despite the circumstances. For example, you never have to give in to sexual harassment. Because you want to understand and participate in as much of the culture as possible, you will probably have to compromise your tastes, traditions, or usual practices. But if you get to know someone really well, then it should become a two-way process, in that both of you share your respective values and things that are important to each of you, even if you are very different from each other.

Inter-cultural Sensitivity

The last thing I want to offer is a **summary of Dr. Milton Bennett's Developmental Model of Intercultural Sensitivity****. This model has helped people to understand how individuals typically tend to approach a new culture, even sometimes unconsciously. It describes a journey between being ethnocentric and ethnorelative. Below are the different stages according to Dr. Bennett, along with my colloquial interpretations:

DENIAL: **Denial against cultural differences**. "I don't really see any differences in this culture. But my culture is the only one that is real to me."

The black and white triangles in the right-hand corner symbolize a person or group of people who see others unlike them as looking all the same, represented by the colorful triangles on the left side of the canvas.

DEFENSE: Defense against cultural differences. "I notice another culture but I don't particularly like the differences. I think ours is the best."

Again, using the black/white triangles, others are seen as people one doesn't like or approve of, sometimes even attacking those others verbally. Here you see some of the others confronting the black/white triangles, but most are moving away to the right side of the canvas.

Going Native: Sometimes this takes the **opposite form where an individual adopts another culture** before they really understand it. They take on all the attributes of that other culture as if it were their own. "Wow, look at me, I have gone native!"

Here the black/white triangles are assuming the characteristics of the local culture, as evidenced by their colorful tails, while the local population gathers around in curiosity, but some even move away in disgust.

MINIMIZATION: **Minimization of cultural differences.** "Okay, I don't really want to focus on the differences, just on how we are alike."

Here there is a better sense of balance as the black/white triangles move through the center, and those around them don't appear to be threatened, but there is no real interaction, positive or negative.

ACCEPTANCE: **Acceptance of cultural differences.** "Now I see that there are many different cultures that are equally real. Mine is only one of them."

Here the black/white triangles are milling around with those of the other culture, beginning to change their colors, and finally accepting them and their culture, even though they are different.

ADAPTATION: **Adaptation of cultural differences**. "So now I am able to see this culture from the perspective of members of that culture. Maybe I will incorporate some of those differences into my own life."

Finally, the black/white triangles become green and white, joining some of the colorful triangles of the other culture, choosing those with whom they feel most connected, starting to move in the same direction.

INTEGRATION: **Integration of cultural differences**. "I can live and work in another culture with a certain amount of ease. I take to heart their worldview, having been influenced by it."

At last, there is full integration of those from both cultures, illustrated by the colors of the rainbow and portraying the fact that we are all multifaceted with many layers.

*Bennett, M.J. (1986) A developmental approach to training for intercultural sensitivity. *International Journal of Intercultural Relations* 10 (2), 179-95. The original reference is: Bennett, J. & Bennett, M. (1975) Description, Interpretation, Evaluation: An Intercultural Exercise in Perception. Teaching material. University of Minnesota, Minneapolis, MN. It is based on ideas from General Semantics and was created as a handout during workshops at the Intercultural Communication Institute in Portland, Oregon. Permission was granted in a phone call between the author and Milton Bennett on April 22, 2022.

**Bennett, M.J. (2004) Becoming Interculturally competent. In J.S. Wurzel (Ed.) *Toward multiculrualism: A reader in multicultural education.* Newton, MA: Intercultural Resource Corporation. This article is also available on Bennett's website: www.idrinstitute.org. Permission granted in a phone call between Milton Bennett and the author, and confirmed in an email that followed on April 22, 2022.

TRAVELING WITH KIDS
IN TROPICAL COUNTRIES

These tips were gathered while our family traveled in Asia together. We didn't figure everything out while traveling, but we did the best we could, and tried to adapt to expressed needs as they surfaced. The suggestions I make here come from my husband, son and daughter, as well as from my own observations and intuition. Most of these tips will work in other environments, even in your own country today, though they developed as we traveled in Asia through the 1980s. Things will have changed to a degree by 2022 and beyond, but some of these suggestions will still work. I should also mention that when we first lived in Sri Lanka, one of our children was seven, the other twelve. When we left nearly three years later, our son was still of elementary age (ten), and our daughter was a teenager (fifteen). In Ghana, our son was fourteen when we arrived, while our daughter was already in college. It was partly this difference in age and gender that inspired many of these suggestions:

A trip is not entirely a vacation. Schedule things for four or five days that you want to be active in experiencing the culture you are traveling in, then take some time off. Taking a weekend for a mini-vacation would be similar to what you would do back home. But in a heavy tourist area, maybe a mid-week break would be better.

For the vacation part of your travels, be a little more lenient about keeping a balanced diet. Allow them to eat ice cream for breakfast if they like. Do some purely fun things that the kids will

234

enjoy without cultural overtones. Move to a fancier hotel/motel with a swimming pool for a couple of days. Give everyone a break. Give the the kids an appropriate allowance to buy stuff they are interested in.

Even though **family economics might require you to share a room** together in a hotel most of the time, sometimes, if safe, let the kids share a separate room. Let the teenager have a room of her own occasionally, while the younger child shares with you. At times, each parent might switch off sharing a room with a child. Alternate. We found one of the most difficult parts of traveling for a couple of months together was too much togetherness. The kids especially got tired and annoyed with each other, which didn't help family dynamics.

If you want to make travel easier, give the kids some responsibility. Give them each a backpack and let them pack their own clothes, suggesting enough for at least a week. This will avoid waiting at baggage claims in most places. If they buy clothes or souvenirs as they travel, they may need to give something away. The alternative would be for them to mail some things home. But many local people appreciate used American clothes. If that sounds tacky, just leave something in the hotel room before you check out, and no doubt someone will find some use for the article of clothing. Every week or ten days we would send our things to the laundry or find someone to pay to wash our clothes. (Be sure that in remote places, if clothes are hand washed, and dried outside on the ground, or on bushes, that they are ironed. This gets rid of the eggs of insects that can irritate.) Also be sure everyone carries a light jacket or sweater for cooler evenings, if appropriate, and a change in shoes. We took a pair of good sneakers and a pair of sandals with us. Jackets/sweaters can be tied around the waist instead of packed. Sometimes they are good on air conditioned planes too.

Allow books to be purchased, one or two at a time. You can find books most anywhere. This gives them something to do—and you too—while waiting in airports, or for a festival to start. When the books are finished, give them away. In most airports, you can find books in English these days, or take kindles with you. Some kids will prefer to do things on their phone instead, which didn't exist when we traveled. Use your judgment as to what is too much, as well as what is best for the trip and the child. Read up on the country you are about to visit, together. Then after the trip, check online or in books to answer any questions, or to learn more.

Encourage everyone to keep a diary, a recording of the trip. It may be a full-blown notebook, or maybe just a few lines a day. As an adult I kept a full notebook and this helped me very much to remember and to write this book. Others in the family may just enjoy reading their diaries again at some point, or share them at some later date with the family, recalling pleasurable experiences.

Except for flights and specific events, don't be to hung up on punctuality. Kids get tired of being hassled to get ready, to hurry. We found that taking the morning easy, having a nice breakfast, or eating at a beach or park, talking and planning our day together was the most calm way to begin it. On the other hand, some families will get up at the crack of dawn, head out, and return for a rest period in the hottest part of the day. Many of the countries we traveled in didn't value punctuality the way that we do anyway, so you all may need to adapt to that as you travel. Also, if anyone is sick, or if it is pouring or hot beyond your comfort zone, change plans. Leave some flexibility in them.

Speaking of plans, **trade-off who gets to choose the next thing to do**. In most instances, you can do more than one thing in the afternoon and evening. Even if others don't like the choice, remind them that they will get their choice next. Amazingly, sometimes they get engaged, with something they were sure they would not like.

Get your kids to use GPS on their phones, or use a map and let them **navigate once in a while**. That way, they have a stake in where they are going.

Encourage your kids to talk with local people as you move around a town or village. If the language is a huge barrier, maybe they can express their interest in what a person is doing by sign or body language, or just by watching, if agreeable to the local person. Kids who don't speak the same language, will often find ways to relate, with a ball, or with music on their phone. Many times those who speak English will seek to talk with you first. You can often learn a lot by asking questions and conversing with them. Some of our best times were with random encounters interacting with people on the street. Of course, you don't want to leave a young child alone with a stranger, but you already know that.

Carry bottled water and snacks for those moments when kids are hungry and thirsty. Sometimes you don't know where next you can get water or food. In out of the way places, buy fruit that can be peeled because it means the insides haven't been handled. Try to avoid buying water in plastic bags on the street, often a little risky. Teach your kids what to look out for in terms of drink and food. Help them to be kind and gracious when they have to say no. Sometimes the easiest drink is just a Coke or Pepsi, without ice.

Staying healthy in general needs to be considered seriously, but not obsessively in public. People will appreciate your trying to interact positively, without complaining or judging. You may want to check online or at the hotel, whether it is safe to go into a lake, river or ocean surf. Be sure to take bug repellent, and anti-malarial pills, if appropriate, and bring other important medications for members of the family with you, if it is not certain whether you can buy them locally. Things have changed since we traveled in Asia, but we tried to drink boiled or bottled water and ate cooked food in places that were off the beaten track. This can assure you that your family will likely stay healthy. Also, be sure to learn ahead about snakes and other critters without freaking out the kids.

Remember the reasons you have chosen to travel in this country. Help your kids to choose events that will shed light on what the local people do best, and how they like to live their lives. Soak up the local culture in music, dance, and theater. They won't easily forget these special experiences. Talk about them afterwards, and process the meaning, if it is unclear to you or them. Ask someone for help in understanding. Take trips into nature, looking for different foliage and flowers, as well as animals. Try to use local transportation whenever possible, to get an idea of the pace of life of the people, whether in a slow rickshaw or a Mercedes Benz taxi.

Remember that every minute of this trip does not have to be filled. This is a shared experience, that you hope everyone will enjoy, but try to avoid planning too much. A variety of unhurried activities, and spare time to rest or read between forays into the culture or countryside worked best for our kids. A few tours can be interesting, but too many, too much history and too many museums can just frustrate younger kids. The same may be true for too much walking. Sometimes spending more time in one location is helpful for everyone to be more relaxed and to process what they are seeing and doing sooner.

As for me, I wanted time together as a family, and time separately, also with each kid, and with my husband. I was willing to alternate those arrangements in each place we stayed. Adventures continue to be important to all of our family, up through today.

GLOSSARY

Adinkra – a woven and stamped cloth with proverbial symbols, called the "goodbye cloth," for mourning in Ghana

Ajowa – a slow expressive dance done by Asante women for public events

Adobo manok – a Filipino dish of chicken marinated in vinegar, soy sauce, garlic, bay leaves and peppercorns, sometimes with the addition of coconut milk

African cloth – a commercially produced cloth with African symbols, as well as some Indonesian designs in bright colors

Agora – open space in ancient Greece for markets and public discussions

Akans – a group of related people in southern Ghana and southeast Ivory Coast, the largest ethnic group in Ghana, with similar languages

Ambahans – traditional poetry inscribed on bamboo pieces by the Hanunoo Mangyans on Oriental Mindoro, the Philippines

Asante – people of the Akan ethnic group, a very powerful confederation from the eighteenth to the early twentieth century

Asantehene – the king of the Asante people

Ate – older sister in Tagalog

Bahasa Indonesia – the official language of Indonesia, based on Malay, which probably originated in northwest Borneo centuries ago.

Bahay kubo – a house on stilts made typically of bamboo with a nipa thatched roof in the Philippines

Baju kurung – an Indonesian outfit

Baklava – a layered filo pastry dessert, filled with walnuts

239

and honey, in Macedonia, origin uncertain, perhaps Persia, but definitely Turkey

Balut – a fertilized duck egg, incubated for eighteen days or more, a delicacy in the Philippines

Banca – a small boat, like a dugout canoe, in the Philippines

Barong tagalog – the long, embroidered shirt created from pineapple or banana leaf fiber in the Philippines. During the Spaniard's colonization, Filipinos were required to wear the shirts outside of their pants, to distinguish them as separate from Spaniards. The shirt is now a traditional dress shirt for Filipino men, and in a different style, for women too.

Barrio – a district of a town in the Philippines

Batik – a molten wax writing or drawing on cotton cloth, which can also be stamped with a metal design, dipped in molten wax, then dyed, in Malaysia and Indonesia, used to create both sarongs and art for the wall

becak – an Indonesian rickshaw created from a bicycle

Beef rendang – rich dish of beef and spices, slow cooked in Malaysia

Beijing – formerly Peiping, capital of China

Bema – podium or platform for oratory in ancient Greece

Benares – located in India, now called Varanasi

Borobudur – a Buddhist monument from the ninth century in Java, Indonesia

Bumiputera – treferring to the Malays, on the Malay peninsula

Burek – a pie made from a flaky dough with a savory filling, often cheese, in Macedonia

Burma – now called Myanmar

Calamansi juice – a tart juice made of a citrus fruit, similar to lime in the Philippines

Calcutta, India – now Kolkata, India

CEDECOM – Central Region Development Commission, Ghana

Cedis – the monetary unit in Ghana, originally cowrie shells

Chadri or burka – a shroud that covers female bodies from head to toe in Afghanistan

Champorado – Filipino chocolate rice porridge

Chana – a dish made from chickpeas in Afghanistan

Cheongsam – a traditional silk dress with high neck and short sleeves, slit at the sides, worn by Chinese women

Chevrons - much prized glass beads with V designs on them, made on Murano Island, Italy, and used for trade beads in Ghana during the Atlantic Slave Trade

China – The People's Republic of China

Chop bar – a casual road-side restaurant in Ghana

Cogon grass – a grass of Asian origin sometimes used for thatch

Crepes suzette – A French dessert pancake served with brandy and citrus juice

Dahan dahan – means slowly and carefully in Tagalog

Dal – nutritious lentil soup in India and Nepal

Dim sum – small Chinese dumplings, savory or sweet, eaten as a snack or a whole meal

Ensaymadas – Filipino bread made from sweet yeast, formed into a spiral pattern and topped with sugar and grated cheese.

Ewe – A people and language from the Volta Region in Ghana

Fufu – a dough pounded from boiled plantains or cassava in Ghana

Gado gado – an Indonesia salad, covered in peanut sauce.

Gamelan – gongs and metal key instruments creating percussionist sounds

Ghana – formerly the Gold Coast Colony of West Africa

Ghats – a flight of steps leading down to a river in India

Guangzhou – formerly Canton, China

Gula melaka – a dessert made from palm sugar in Malaysia

Gung ho – American slang based on the Chinese word for energetic or enthusiastic

Gye nyame – the most important proverbial symbol in Ghana, meaning "except for god," referring to the omnipotence of god

Harmattan – a wind off of the Sahara Desert which blows down to the coast of Ghana from December to February

Hokkien – a Chinese dialect

Hong Kong – now Hong Kong Special Administration Region

of China

Ikan merah – cooked red snapper in Malaysia

Jalan Datu – jalan = street, datu = king, in Malaysia

Jeepney – a jitney bus converted from an American jeep after WWII in the Philippines

Jesselton – now Kota Kinabalu, Sabah, Malaysia

Jitneys – unlicensed taxi in Asia

kaba and slit – fitted top and fitted long skirt with a slit, worn by women in Ghana

Kain – cloth wrapped around the hips of both men and women in Malaysia, usually down to the ankles

Kamben – a torso wrap for women, covering the chest in Indonesia

Kampong – a rural village in Malaysia

Kari ayam – chicken curry in Malaysia

Kari ikan – fish curry in Malaysia

Kebaya – a loose tunic worn by women in Southeast Asia, often lacy

Kenkey – a fermented sour dough dumpling made of corn in Ghana

Kente – a finely woven strip cloth created on moveable looms, traditionally by men in Ghana who also sew the strips together to form a large cloth for men or women

Kentehene – commercially woven cloth to resemble handwoven kente in Ghana

Khow suey – noodle soup in spiced coconut milk in Burma

Kilims – flat woven tapestries for the floor, woven from as far away as Mongolia, but definitely in the former Ottoman Empire of current Turkey, also in Macedonia and other nearby countries

Kiri bath – rice cake cooked with coconut milk in Sri Lanka

KL – Kuala Lumpur, Malaysia

Kofi Brokeman – roasted ripe plaintains accompanied by roasted ground nuts, a nutritious snack in Ghana

Kota Bharu – city in Malaysia

Kris – an Indonesian dagger with a wavy-edged blade

Krupuk – a prawn cracker originating in Southeast Asia

Kuya – older brother in Tagalog

Kway teow – rice noodle dish in Malaysia (originally Hokkien, in China)

Lamprais – a combination of meat, spices, and rice packaged together in banana leaves in Sri Lanka

Longyi – cloth worn around the waist and hips in Burma

Love cake – a semolina cake with rosewater, cashews and spices in Sri Lanka

Lumpia – spring rolls, fresh or fried, in the Philippines

Macedonia – now called the Republic of North Macedonia

Mangyan – An ethnic group living in the mountains of Oriental Mindoro in the Philippines, pronounced *mun yun*

Masala thosai – a savory, crisp pancake sometimes stuffed with vegetables and dipped in sauces, in Sri Lanka (from southern India)

Millefiori – "a thousand flowers," a style of blown glass beads created on Murano Island, Italy, used for trade in Ghana during the Atlantic Slave Trade

Moussaka – eggplant or potato dish which includes meat, originally from Turkey, but also found in Macedonia.

MUCIA – Midwest University Consortium for International Activities, in Ghana

Mulligatawny – a spicy soup with curry flavor and coconut milk in Sri Lanka, originally Indian

Nasi biriyani – rice cooked with spices, and meat, vegetables, chicken or fish, served on a banana leaf in Malaysia

New Hebrides – now Vanuatu

Nkatenkwan – ground nut soup in Ghana, eaten with fufu

Obroni – white person or foreigner in Ghana

Ohrid – refers to a huge spring-fed lake between eastern Albania and southwestern Macedonia, also the name of the town next to it

Orang puteh – literally, white man in Malaysia

Pagan – now Bagan in Burma

Palaver – to talk at length, to negotiate, in Ghana the auction block

Pan de sal – bread baked in the Philippines for breakfast (salt bread, literally)

Panafest – a festival of music, dance and theater started in 1992 in Cape Coast, Ghana, performed every two years to celebrate the heritage and cultures of the African continent and its Diaspora

Pancit – a noodle dish in the Philippines

Papadam – deep fried black gram bean flour in Sri Lanka

Papua, New Guinea –now Papua

Paratha and naan – Indian flat breads

Pastrmalija – a rustic bread pie, topped with cubed meat, resembling pizza, in Macedonia

PCV – Peace Corps Volunteer

Pittu – steamed cylinder of ground rice with coconut in Sri Lanka

Prambanan – a Hindu monument from the ninth century in Java, Indonesia

President Aquino – assassinated at Manila airport in 1986. His wife, Corazon, ran for president of the Philippines afterwards.

Rakija – fruit brandy in Macedonia

Ramayana – an Indian story of Prince Rama, trying to get his wife, Sita, way from Ravanna, with the help of monkeys

Ramie – fabric made from a flowering plant in the Philippines

Rangoon – now Yangon, capital of Myanmar, formerly Burma

Reyna Elena – someone personifying St. Helena in the Flores de Mayo festival in the Philippines

Rijstaffel – created by Dutch plantation owners in Indonesia, meaning "rice table"

Roma – formerly called 'gypsies', now considered a perjorative term, the former term possibly originating from a connection to Egypt, but now probably referring to people who migrated out of India approximately 1,000 years ago

Rostrum – a platform for a speech in Rome

Roti chanai – pan fried flat bread, repeatedly folded with ghee in Malaysia

RPCV – Returned Peace Corps Volunteer

Sahel – semi-arid area between the savanna and the Sahara Desert

Salwar Kameez – a woman's garment, composed of a loose tunic over loose pants, sewed tightly at the ankles, worn in India

Saree – up to nine yards of silk or cotton, wrapped and pleated around the waist of a woman, one end draped over the arm in Sri Lanka and India

Sate – grilled meat with spices, on a stick in Malaysia

Savanna – a dry area with stand alone trees and tall grass in Ghana

Shopska salata – a salad of chopped greens, cucumbers, tomatoes, onion, peppers, topped with a white cheese in Macedonia and other Balkan countries.

Short eats – snacks or appetizers in Sri Lanka

Sip saawng – the number twelve in the Thai language

SIT – School for International Training, Brattleboro, Vermont

Sri Lanka – formerly known as the country of Ceylon

Stringhoppers – rice flour squeezed through a press and steamed in Sri Lanka

Tagalog – principal language spoken in Central Luzon, similar to Filipino, the national language in the Philippines

Tandoor – a cylindrical oven used to cook meat and poultry in northern India

Tavce gravce – a Macedonia form of baked beans

The Silk Road – an exchange of goods along a route from China to Italy, starting in about the second century BCE, following an earlier route started by Alexander the Great of Greece, in the fourth century BC that didn't quite make it to China

Tjanting – the slender metal tool that enables Indonesian artists to draw with molten wax on cotton cloth to create a resist before dying

Tjap – a copper stamp made into a design which, when dipped into molten wax, transfers that design as a resist on cotton cloth in Indonesia and Malaysia

Trincomalee – a port city in Sri Lanka, on the eastern coast

Tri-shaws – cycle rickshaws in Malaysia

Twi – an Akan language spoken by the Asantes in Ghana

Ular – snake in the Malay language

USAID – United States Agency for International Development

Watalappam – a dense custard of coconut and jaggary (cane juice and palm sap) in Sri Lanka

Wayang kulit – a shadow play with leather puppets telling old tales from the Indian Maharabata and the Ramayana, performed in the former Indian empires in the East Indies, and continuing under the name of Indonesia

Western Samoa – now the country of Samoa

Yuan – the Chinese unit for money